Business information sys
Volume 2
Systems Analysis and Design

By Graham C Lester, BSc(Econ), MBCS
Senior Lecturer in Computer Studies
Department of Business Information Technology
Faculty of Management and Business
Manchester Polytechnic

PITMAN
PUBLISHING

PITMAN PUBLISHING
128 Long Acre, London WC2E 9AN

A Division of Longman Group Limited

© Longman Group UK Limited 1992

Third edition published as *Data Processing Volume 2* in Great Britain 1988
This edition first published in Great Britain 1992
Reprinted 1993, 1994

British Library Cataloguing in Publication Data
A catalogue record for this book is available from the British Library

ISBN 0–273–03807–9

Typeset in 10/12pt Times by Mathematical Composition Setters Ltd, Salisbury, UK
Printed in Singapore

For
Catherine Helen, Oliver Charles
and Emma Laura

Contents

Preface

This book provides a comprehensive introductory course of study for those wishing to gain an understanding of the computer, and of the role of the computer in commercial data processing. The book is divided into two volumes:

Volume 1 gives an introduction to the scope and subject matter of data processing, explaining what a computer is and how it is programmed. To put this material into perspective, the volume ends with a chapter which outlines the tasks undertaken by the systems analyst.

Volume 2 deals in detail with the role of the systems analyst and with his work. The implications of computer use are also discussed.

The book is suitable for students who are preparing themselves for data processing examinations set by the following bodies:

The Chartered Association of Certified Accountants (ACCA)
The British Computer Society (BCS)
The Chartered Institute of Public Finance and Accountancy (CIPFA)
The Association of Accounting Technicians (AAT)
The Institute of Chartered Accountants in England and Wales (ICA)
The Institute of Cost and Management Accountants (ICMA)

In addition, it is suitable for those taking data processing papers on BTEC Certificate and Diploma courses, and on degree courses.

Each chapter ends with a set of typical examination questions and, at the end of those chapters where it is appropriate, a series of questions is set to test the reader's understanding of what has been presented. These questions should be attempted 'unseen' and readers should satisfy themselves, by reference to the answers to selected questions in the Appendix at the end of the volume, that they have understood the subject matter of a chapter before proceeding.

Volume 1 also contains an extensive glossary in Appendix 1.

I wish to acknowledge the permission to use past examination papers granted by the Chartered Association of Certified Accountants, the Association of Accounting Technicians, the Institute of Chartered Accountants in England and Wales, and the Chartered Institute of Management Accountants.

Acknowledgement

I should like to thank my wife Linda for typing what follows, and for help and encouragement during the writing and the revision of this book.

Unit Four

Systems analysis and design

17

The work of the systems analyst

17.1 The place of the analyst

We saw in Chapter 1 of Volume 1 that the usual sequence of events when a user, or customer, requires an area of work to be computerized is as shown in Fig 17.1.

Now that we have looked at what the computer is, what it is capable of doing, and the way it is programmed, we are in a position to examine more closely the work of the systems analyst. Such an examination is the function of this fourth unit.

The reader should carefully note that, in this unit, we assume

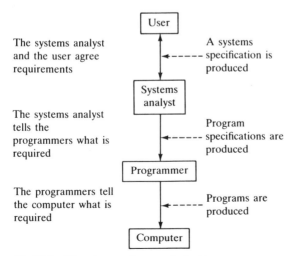

Fig 17.1   The stages of computerization

that the systems analyst is working for an organization which uses a main-frame computer, and that the organization's machine is already being used successfully in other areas of the organization's business. The analyst is thus *not* being asked to decide whether or not a computer should be acquired – that decision has already been made. We shall look at the problems of computer acquisition later.

17.2   The stages of systems analysis

The steps which a systems analyst has to undertake in order to computerize an area of an organization's business are dealt with in detail in the remainder of this unit.

We will begin with an overall look at the 'traditional' way in which systems analysts have developed business systems over the last 30 or so years. This will allow the individual steps to be placed into context as we come across them. We shall then examine the problems which are posed by this approach, and at methodologies which attempt to overcome those problems.

1   The first stage of any systems work is to determine the area of the business which is to be the subject of the study. This should be communicated to the systems analyst in a formal, written, document which acts as the **terms of reference**.

2   Having been given those terms of reference, the analyst has next to determine whether or not a full study into the area in question would be worth while. In order to do this a **project feasibility study** has to be carried out to estimate the likely costs and benefits of the proposed system. At the end of the study, the analyst produces a **project feasibility report** which recommends whether or not the systems study should continue.

3   If the project feasibility study recommends that the project should go ahead, and if it is accepted, then a **full systems study** is carried out. This will involve:

- a **fact finding** exercise which entails a detailed examination of the area of business under review
- **recording** the facts found so that they can be referred to during the subsequent stages
- examination and **analysis** of the recorded facts in an attempt to identify the strengths and weaknesses of the current system, and in order to determine what will be required of the new system. At this stage, a **statement of requirements** is often produced

● **design** of a new, improved system of data processing which meets the user's needs. The design will be embodied in a document called a **systems specification**. Once again, likely costs and benefits will feature in this report

4   If the systems specification which the analyst has produced is accepted, then the proposed system will need to be programmed. To allow this to happen, the analyst prepares a **program specification** for each program which the programmers are to write. The programs are then written and tested by the programmers concerned. The analyst usually works in conjunction with a senior programmer to supervise this phase of the project and to ensure that the programmers work to the required standards.

5   Once programs have been written and tested individually, **system testing** can take place. At this point, all the programs are tested together to ensure that they function correctly as an entity, and that they interface with one another, and with the clerical systems which support them. Any errors found at this stage will, of course, be corrected, and the process of testing repeated.

6   Once a system has been thoroughly tested and the personnel concerned feel that it is robust, all the **documentation** relating to it must be brought up-to-date. This will include all specifications and flowcharts, and it will also mean that the analyst has to produce various manuals, so that the staff who are expected to run the system are made aware of what is required of them. Examples are the operations manual, written for the computer operators, and the user procedure manual, written for the clerical staff in the affected department(s).

7   The new system can then be **implemented**. This involves:

● creating a new master file either from scratch or, more likely, by converting an existing manual file, or computer file
● changing over, in a carefully-planned fashion, to the new computerized procedures

Some months after implementation has taken place, it will be necessary to review the live system, so that its actual performance can be evaluated against the targets set earlier. A post-implementation review report will be produced.

8   The analyst's work does not come to an end when a new system has been implemented. Throughout its operational life, a computer system needs to be diligently **maintained**. Periodic reviews of the

system in operation will have to be made, to ensure that it is still meeting its objectives.

17.3 Planning and monitoring a project

Because of the high cost of using a computer, and the high salaries paid to computer personnel, it is imperative that all computer projects should be meticulously planned. When the project feasibility report is produced, estimates should be made of the effort required for the development of the system, and the total costs involved. When the systems specification is written, more detailed estimates must be made.

As further work is undertaken, progress should be monitored against these estimates so that deviations can be highlighted. The use of periodic progress meetings, where the analysts have to answer to their management, perhaps on a monthly basis, will facilitate this. Such monitoring will allow the appropriate corrective action to be taken, and it will allow the user to be informed of any significant changes, to target dates or costs, which are anticipated.

Where appropriate, such control tools as Gantt charts or network analysis should be employed.

17.4 Assumptions made

The reader will appreciate that there are few 'rules' in systems analysis and design. Each computer installation has its own accepted way of working and, to some extent, each individual within each installation 'does his own thing'. In what follows, one way of carrying out the tasks which need to be tackled in order to design and implement a computer system is given.

In particular, the next part of this unit assumes, for the sake of clarity, that only one analyst is involved. This may well be the case in the development of a small or medium-sized system, but it will not be the case where a large system is involved. In such circumstances a team of systems analysts, headed by a project manager, will be given the responsibility of developing the system, and the team members will work together to investigate, design and implement it.

Another approach is to have different individuals, or teams, carrying out the successive stages of systems development; one team may investigate and hand its findings on to another, which designs.

A further point that the reader should bear in mind is that much of what follows assumes that there is a present system which needs to be replaced. This is often, but not always, the case in practice; where it does not apply, the analyst will have to alter the approach somewhat.

Finally the reader should bear in mind the fact that the stages in systems development are presented in chronological sequence as if one step followed carefully upon the last. In actual practice, the steps overlap and, sometimes, are tackled in a different sequence.

17.5 Summary

The various stages involved in computerizing an area of an organization's operations are shown below. In each case, the end-product(s) of the stage is shown.

Stage	End-product
Determining the area of work	Terms of reference
Determining feasibility	Project feasibility report
Systems investigation	Statement of requirements
Systems design	Systems specification
Systems development	Program specifications
	Programs
	Manuals
Implementation	An operational system
Maintenance	Post-implementation review report
	Periodic review reports

Examination questions

1 Assume that you are a systems analyst with XYZ Ltd. A computer has been installed and satisfactory computerized payroll and sales accounting systems are now in operation. It has been agreed that the next project will be to transfer the company's raw material stock control system to the computer. Outline the main stages through which you would expect the project to pass. It is not expected that any additional computing equipment will be required.

2 (a) What are the principal duties of a systems analyst during the life of a systems project?

(b) Outline the personal qualities required by the systems analyst in carrying out his work.

(Chartered Association of Certified Accountants)

18

Systems investigation

18.1 Introduction

This chapter examines the work of the systems analyst during the systems investigation phase.

Working from a written terms of reference, the analyst thoroughly investigates the current system and carefully analyses the findings. At the end of the investigation, the analyst produces a statement of requirements which should be approved by personnel in the affected department(s) or section(s) before any further work is undertaken.

18.2 The terms of reference

In organizations which are not well-managed, areas of work are computerized in a haphazard fashion. Ideas concerning potential computerization come from line departments which find that their work load has grown so much that they cannot cope under present arrangements, from functional specialists such as organization and methods officers who perceive a need for computerized processing in a certain area, from top management who have read about computers or attended courses which contain a computing element, and from various other sources. Clearly, this approach is far from satisfactory.

In a well-run organization, on the other hand, a committee of senior personnel guides the work of the computer department, according to a long-range, predetermined, plan of action. This high-level **steering committee** will attempt to ensure that areas of the organization's work are computerized in a logical sequence, so that maximum savings can be made. As one project is completed, and resources are released, the next project on the list will begin.

When a project is due to be started, a formal, written, terms of reference should be agreed between the user department and the data processing department. This document is known by several names, among them **project brief** and **initial assignment brief** but, whatever it is called in a given organization, it should cover the following points:

- the title of the project
- the subject of the study
- the purpose and scope of the study
- the personnel and the department(s) or section(s) involved
- any constraints which the analyst will have to work to
- the timescales involved
- the resources available to the analyst
- any other information deemed relevant

Many organizations initiate projects on a standardized, pre-printed form.

18.3 The project feasibility study

18.3.1 The nature of the project feasibility study

Armed with the terms of reference, the systems analyst can now begin the project feasibility study.

In the early days of computing, it was often necessary to determine whether it was possible, or feasible, to carry out a given task on a computer, and a feasibility study would be carried out with this in mind. This is no longer usually the case, however, because, as the reader will by now have realized, any task which can be unambiguously defined can be performed by the machine. What we need to determine today, before we commit resources to the computerization of any area of business, is whether it is worth doing the job by computer. The study which an analyst carries out to answer this question should perhaps thus be called a project justification study; in practice it still tends to be called a **project feasibility study.**

Note carefully that, in this chapter, we are not talking about the initial feasibility study which an organization carries out in conjunction with the manufacturers of computer equipment to determine whether or not a computer should be acquired: we are assuming that a computer is already being used by the organization concerned. The computer feasibility study which is carried out to determine whether a computer should be acquired is dealt with later, in Unit 6.

18.3.2 The aims of the project feasibility study

A properly-conducted project feasibility study will thus achieve the following aims:

1 It will allow the organization's management to decide whether or not to commit further resources to a project, by showing whether or not a full systems study appears to be justified. The anticipated costs and benefits of the new system will thus be an important part of the project feasibility report.
2 It will outline the present system and summarize its costs. Any problems in the present system will be highlighted.
3 It will outline the proposed new system, and justify it in cost terms.
4 It will provide a standard against which future performance can be monitored.
5 It will form the basis of the terms of reference which will be given to the systems analyst who is to conduct the full systems study.

18.3.3 Carrying out the project feasibility study

A project feasibility study is, in effect, a miniature systems study. Facts about the present system are found and recorded, so that they can be analysed. An outline design of the new system can then be attempted. Estimates of the costs and benefits of the new system can be made.

18.3.4 The project feasibility report

At the end of the project feasibility study, a project feasibility report is produced. It should contain the following sections:

1 An **introduction** to the study. This should reflect the contents of the initial terms of reference.

2 A description of the **existing system**, with particular reference to any problems and difficulties which can be identified, and to the costs of running the present system.

3 The **proposed new system** should be outlined, using system flowcharts, and the input to the system, the master file(s) maintained and the output produced should be described.

4 The proposals should be **justified**, the cost, both development and running costs, and the benefits of the new system being quantified in financial terms.

5 A **development plan** for the proposed system should be drawn up, showing the stages involved in its implementation, and the resources required.

6 **Recommendations**, as to the next steps to be taken, should be made by the systems analyst.

18.3.5 The first major decision point

The recommendations in the project feasibility report will then have to be considered. Copies should be sent to:

- the prospective 'user' of the computer department's services, the management of the section(s) or department(s) whose work it is proposed to computerize
- the management of the data processing department
- the steering committee
- representatives of the finance function
- the auditors

If a decision to go ahead with the full systems study is made, then new terms of reference, sometimes known as the **final assignment brief**, will have to be prepared for the systems analyst who is to carry it out. This second brief will contain the same information as the first, *see* 18.2, but in an updated form relating to the full study.

The full systems study can then begin.

18.4   Fact finding

18.4.1   The objectives of the fact finding stage

The first stage in a full systems study, once the project feasibility report has been accepted, is fact finding. During the fact finding stage, the systems analyst should attempt to discover information about the present system under the following headings:

1   The **objectives** and **scope** of the system; what is the present system attempting to accomplish?

2   The **input** to the system; what form is the input in when it enters the system; where does it originate; what items are included in the input? In addition, the systems analyst will be concerned about the volumes of input entering the system, as these may well have a direct bearing on the design of the new system; what are the minimum, average and maximum volumes of input; does this input peak at certain times; is it likely to grow over time?

3   The **files maintained** by the present system will also interest the analyst who will need to ascertain such details as the frequency of file updating and the nature of any coding systems which are used.

4   The nature and contents of the **output** from the system; what form is the output in; how often is it produced; what purpose is it put to; is it necessary?

5   The **processing** carried out by the system; how is the input used to update the files and produce the output; what equipment, if any, is used; what accuracy checks are performed during processing; are there any time constraints; what happens to exceptional items?

6   The **organization structure** of the department(s) or section(s) presently carrying out the processing, and the **personnel** involved.

7   The **problems** and **difficulties** presently encountered as the system operates will need to be highlighted, with special reference to bottlenecks, duplication and weaknesses.   ·

8   The **costs** of the present system will need to be known.

In addition to finding facts about the present system, the analyst should attempt to ascertain what information, **under ideal circumstances**, management would like to receive from the system – improvement is, after all, what the analyst is trying to achieve.

18.4.2 Meeting and overcoming resistance

The finding and verification of all relevant facts concerning a data processing system, as outlined before, is clearly a major objective of the fact finding stage. It is not, however, the only objective. Most human beings are creatures of habit who dislike change, and this dislike often manifests itself at their place of work. And yet the computer, with which the analyst is concerned, is nothing if it is not the agent of change. So far as many of the clerical staff are concerned, therefore, the systems analyst represents change, being the 'personification' of the computer. These considerations will often lead to a situation at the start of a systems investigation where resistance, suspicion and fear are rife.

It is a crucial objective of the analyst during the investigation phase, then, to meet and overcome these feelings. If this is done successfully, and an atmosphere of trust is created, then it is possible to enlist the co-operation of the personnel with whom the analyst will be working throughout the life of the systems project. This can only have beneficial results so far as the project, and all involved with it, are concerned.

18.4.3 Methods of fact finding

Facts about existing systems can be gathered by using one or more of the following techniques:

- reading records and documentation relating to the system
- sending questionnaires to personnel involved in the present system
- interviewing relevant members of staff
- observation of the system in operation

Of course, not all of these methods will be appropriate in every set of circumstances. The systems analyst should use those techniques which, when used in combination, allow the gathering of the maximum amount of relevant information about the system in the minimum amount of time, consistent with the human relations considerations outlined above. Perhaps reading documentation followed by the design and distribution of a questionnaire could be used by an analyst prior to the conducting of interviews.

18.4.4   Reading around the system

The existing records and documents which relate to a system which is being investigated will often prove to be a useful starting point for an analyst's fact finding work. The following can be consulted:

- organization charts which depict the formal structure of the organization's relevant parts
- procedures manuals, job descriptions and job specifications which lay down how tasks should be carried out
- the forms used within the system
- the files which the system maintains
- the output which the system produces
- any other documentation which is generated by the system; reports, statistical summaries, memoranda, letters, handbooks and training aids, for example

From such a study, the systems analyst would hope to gain a background knowledge of the system, the personnel involved with it, and the problems and difficulties encountered in its operation. This should permit the analyst to direct the subsequent fact finding in the correct direction; in short, the analyst will be able to ask the 'right' questions. This will expedite the investigation phase, and help convince the user department staff that they are dealing with a competent professional.

When inspecting documentation, however, the analyst should bear the following points in mind:

1   Such documents as organization charts and procedures manuals can only show the official state of affairs. Often, in practice, modifications are made by the staff who carry out processing tasks within a system. Such alternations will not be shown in the system's formal documentation.

2   Because human systems are dynamic, written documentation becomes out-of-date over time. Even where a chart or a specification was once an accurate representation of a situation, this will not normally be the case for any length of time.

3   Reading all the documents relating to the operation of a system will be a time-consuming and expensive task; the analyst must be selective.

4   Once a background knowledge has been gained, the analyst must remember that it is no more than that. The analyst must attempt to confirm that the learned facts are in fact true, and resist the temptation to flaunt the newly-found knowledge in front of staff in the user department; nothing, after all, could antagonize them more.

18.4.5 The use of questionnaires

When an analyst needs to gather information from a large number of people, the use of a carefully-prepared questionnaire may be appropriate. When considering the use of this technique, the following points should be borne in mind:

1 Questionnaires save the analyst's time and, therefore, save money during the investigation phase, especially if answers are required from a large number of people; the high overhead of preparing a questionnaire will not normally be worth while when small numbers are involved.

2 This cost saving will be increased when the respondents are geographically spread.

3 The questionnaire method best lends itself to situations where simple yes/no answers, or straightforward answers such as 'twice a week' or '379 per annum' are appropriate; the method is not too helpful where opinions, suggestions or complaints are being looked for.

4 Following on from point 3, the questionnaire suffers from the disadvantage of not allowing face-to-face communications; a respondent cannot ask the author of a questionnaire exactly what is meant in a question! Similarly, the following up of interesting areas which are half-uncovered in a questionnaire will be slow and, perhaps, costly.

5 Questionnaires must be very meticulously thought out in an attempt to avoid ambiguous questions. Despite efforts made in this direction, however, some answers usually prove useless because the questions have been misunderstood. Where possible, a questionnaire should be tested on a small sample of respondents before it is used in the field.

6 Response to a survey carried out using questionnaires usually proves slow, the temptation to delay answering the questionnaire proving too great for many respondents; this can severely hinder the analyst's investigation.

7 After replies have been received, their analysis takes time and may prove costly.

8   The response to a given survey, using this method, may prove low.

9   If the conduct of the survey itself is not carefully planned, the use of questionnaires may antagonize those to whom they are sent. At the very least, a well-worded introductory letter is called for.

18.4.6   Face-to-face interviews

The face-to-face interview with members of staff of the department(s) or section(s) involved in the administration of the existing system is the most common method of fact gathering employed by systems analysts. Once again, there are certain considerations which should be borne in mind when this method is being used:

1   The interviews which take place must fit into the analyst's overall fact finding strategy. This will ensure that a basic background knowledge has been gained, perhaps from reading or the use of questionnaires, before any conversation is begun. It will also ensure that the right people are interviewed, in the right sequence; this will allow the correct questions to be asked of each person, as it is little use asking a clerk what the department's five-year plans are, just as it will probably prove unrewarding to ask a manager a very detailed question about a clerical function which his/her staff are responsible for.

2   Before interviews are commenced, the interviewees must be made aware of the purpose of the investigation; a presentation which involves a senior manager in the department concerned may well be the best way to allay the fears and suspicions which will naturally arise in such circumstances.

3   Individual interviews should be arranged well in advance, to allow a suitable time to be chosen. Busy periods of the week or month, or sessions immediately prior to lunch, should be avoided, for example.

4   The correct place for the interview should be selected. If the interview takes place at the analyst's desk, then the interviewee may be unforthcoming, not being on familiar territory and, perhaps, feeling 'summoned' by the analyst. On the other hand, an interview at the other party's place of work may lead to interruptions and, possibly, to a lack of confidentiality, although an advantage will be gained from the fact that the interviewee will have all documentation to hand. Clearly, a decision on the location of an interview will have to be carefully taken; perhaps 'neutral territory' may be the answer.

5 The conduct of the interview itself will be all-important. Of course, the analyst must observe the usual rules of politeness, and choose a terminology and language appropriate to the interviewee. The analyst must also be unbiased and objective throughout.

6 The structure of the interview will vary depending on the circumstances of an individual case but, in general, the following pattern often proves useful:

● an initial phase when the two parties involved become accustomed to each other and overcome their preliminary awkwardness

● the main part of the interview when the real fact finding takes place. A previously-prepared list of questions, with plenty of space for answers to be entered, is usually helpful, although the analyst must be prepared to be flexible as unexpected topics are broached. The analyst should endeavour to encourage the interviewee who is finding self-expression difficult, but should avoid leading questions, such as those which begin 'do you always ...'. A useful technique is for the analyst to describe back to the interviewee what they **think** the interviewee has said; they will not always have understood a complex procedure correctly, after all

● a final phase of the interview, in which the analyst should allow the interviewee to raise any further points which the analyst may have missed. This part of the interview is often fruitful, and, if nothing else, it conveys to the interviewee the fact that the analyst feels his/her opinions are worth asking for.

7 The analyst should take careful notes during the interview and these should be written up as soon after the end of the session as is possible; delay may make the notes unintelligible. Many analysts send a copy of their summary of an interview to the person concerned for confirmation; errors will be highlighted by this process.

18.4.7 Observation

However truthful interviewees or respondents to a questionnaire attempt to be, they can only inform the systems analyst of what they believe to be the state of affairs in a given set of circumstances. Clearly, what actually happens may well differ quite fundamentally in practice. For this reason, and because, in certain situations, there is a possibility of deliberate misrepresentation, the analyst may use observation as a fact finding method. Observation overcomes these problems by allowing the analyst to see with his own eyes what is happening in a department. In particular, the analyst can find out how often staff are interrupted in their work, what sort of pressures they are under, what their relationships with colleagues, their attitudes to the work, the supervision and the organization are like, and how often and for how long they do tasks other than those they are supposed to! Obviously, these facts will be difficult to come by in an interview, and yet they may be most important to the analyst's subsequent work.

The problems posed by observation as a fact finding technique are three-fold. Firstly, observation will take a lot of time; this means that it is costly and that the development of the new system is hindered. Secondly, observation may antagonize staff who dislike being 'spied' upon. Thirdly, the behaviour of those being observed may, consciously or unconsciously, be modified when the analyst is in attendance; the observer of a system does indeed become an integral part of that system.

In an attempt to overcome these difficulties, several different approaches may be tried. On the one hand, activity sampling may be used. This is a statistical technique which allows the observer to make a small number of random observations of activities which are taking place, rather than a continuous observation. Another solution is to give the analyst a desk in the affected department to do some of the work there. All the analyst will need to do then is to keep his or her eyes and ears open!

18.5 Fact recording

18.5.1 The need for systematic fact recording

As a systems analyst carries out a lengthy fact finding exercise, much information about the existing system will be accumulated. A good deal of that information, however, will be held in a rather haphazard form; the analyst will have, inter alia, notes taken during interviews, samples of forms used, and a varied collection of charts and manuals.

Clearly, such documentation will only be of use to the analyst for a given length of time. After several weeks or months have elapsed, the significance of a scribbled note in the margin of a form, or on a chart, will be diminished or, worse still, lost. And yet the system investigation phase is supposed to be the basis for the rest of the analyst's work!

The answer to this problem is that the analyst must systematically record the facts found, as the investigation is carried out. The fact finding and fact recording phases are thus carried out in parallel; as facts are uncovered, they have to be documented.

Many fact recording techniques are available to the systems analyst, and, in a given set of circumstances, those which are most appropriate will have to be carefully selected. In all cases, however, a formal systems file, or project file, should be maintained so that:

- individual facts can be retrieved when required
- individual facts can be placed into the overall context of the total system
- all recorded facts can be efficiently used in the subsequent stages of the analyst's work

Several of the fact recording methods which an analyst may utilize are dealt with in the remainder of this section.

18.5.2   Narrative

A narrative description is often a convenient method of recording facts. Narrative can be used, for example, to describe the structure of the department(s) or section(s) carrying out a processing task, to give a picture of the forms and records used, or to detail the processing steps carried out. The use of narrative, however, may be time-consuming and, because of the inherent ambiguity of any natural language, confusing. For these reasons, formalized diagrams, tabulations and charts are often used to support narrative.

18.5.3   Recording staff details

An organization chart is the commonest method of showing the staff involved in a particular data processing task, and their relationships. Where charts are already available, they should be utilized by the systems analyst, but the points made about them under fact finding (18.4) should be borne in mind. Where no charts, or only hopelessly out-of-date charts, are available, the analyst should construct them personally.

An example of an organization chart is shown in Fig 18.1. This can be supplemented by a **staff deployment form**, which summarizes the numbers of staff of different levels who are employed in each department (*see* Fig 18.2). Further detail can be recorded on a job description form (*see* Fig 18.3).

The time spent during the week by an employee on different tasks can be recorded on a **time utilization form** (*see* Fig 18.4).

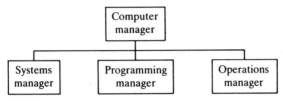

Fig 18.1   Part of an organization chart

	STAFF DEPLOYMENT FORM			
Project name:	XYZ			
Analyst:	A.N. OTHER			
Date:	010499			

Dept/ section	Managers	Supervision	Staff	Total
AAA	1	6	14	21
BBC	1	4	11	16
CCC	1	5	12	18
Totals	3	15	37	55

Fig 18.2   The staff deployment form

JOB DESCRIPTION FORM
Project name: **Analyst:** **Date:**
Job title:
Reference:
Responds to:
Subordinate staff:
Responsibilities:

Fig 18.3   The job description form

TIME UTILIZATION FORM	
Project name: **Analyst:** **Date:**	
Job title: **Reference:**	
Task	**Hours spent**
Total	
Remarks:	

Fig 18.4   The time utilization form

18.5.4   The form description document

When an analyst is recording facts about the operation of an existing data processing system, the forms which are used within that system are examined very closely. Because of this, copies of each of those forms, both blank copies and copies with sample data entered, will be filed.

The forms themselves, even those with sample data entered on them, cannot tell the whole story, however; they cannot give information about the maximum, average and minimum values found in certain fields, for instance. To supplement sample forms, then, the analyst should complete a **form description document**, which does carry such information. An example of a form description document is shown in Fig 18.5.

FORM DESCRIPTION DOCUMENT	
Project name: **Analyst:** **Date:**	
Title of document:	
Usually known as:	
Purpose:	
Originated:	
Used by:	
Destination:	

Number of copies – minimum average maximum	} per
Variations	

Field name	Size	Comments

Remarks:

Fig 18.5   *A form description document*

Clearly, the use of a pre-printed document such as Fig 18.5 will force the analyst to remember to discover all the pertinent facts about a form.

18.5.5   The file description document

The files used within a system also have to be described. A file description document, such as the one shown in Fig 18.6, allows this to be done. The document is used in conjunction with the record description document, which is outlined in the next subsection.

FILE DESCRIPTION DOCUMENT
Project name: Analyst: Date:
Name of file:
Purpose:
Records in file:
Maintenance:
Volumes:
Remarks:

Fig 18.6   A file description document

18.5.6   The record description document

For each record named on a file description document, a record description document should be made out. This should look something like the form shown in Fig 18.7.

18.5.7   The clerical procedures flowchart

When recording the processing steps carried out within a system, an analyst may use many different techniques. In this subsection and the next two, we look at three of those techniques – the clerical procedures flowchart, the data flow diagram and the decision table.

RECORD DESCRIPTION DOCUMENT				
Project name: **Analyst:** **Date:**				
Name of record:				
Name of file:				
Field	**Format**	**Max. size**	**Ave. size**	**Remarks**
Notes:				

Fig 18.7 *A record description document*

There are no generally-accepted conventions which govern the drawing of clerical procedures flowcharts. In what follows we describe one method which is in common use. The symbols employed are shown in Fig 18.8.

These symbols are combined to depict diagrammatically the processes which are carried out. Thus, the receipt of a purchase requisition, its checking, and the entering of an invalid requisition routine when an error arises, would be shown as in Fig 18.9.

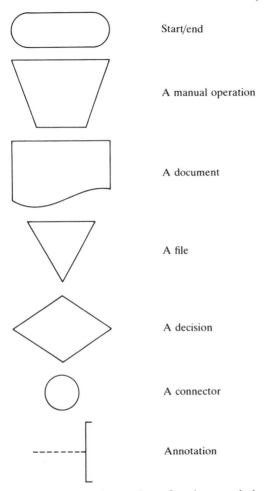

Start/end

A manual operation

A document

A file

A decision

A connector

Annotation

Fig 18.8   Clerical procedures flowchart symbols

The copying of details from a supplier delivery note onto a three-part goods received document and its subsequent chronological filing, would be shown as in Fig 18.10.

The searching of a purchase order file for a copy of a particular order is shown in Fig 18.11.

An order routine is described below. The reader should attempt to draw a clerical procedures flowchart which depicts the routine. The exercise should be attempted before the chart shown in Fig 18.12 is consulted.

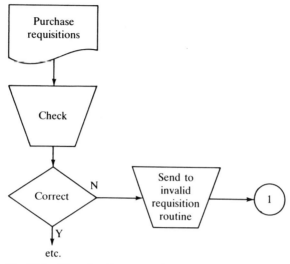

Fig 18.9 The checking operation

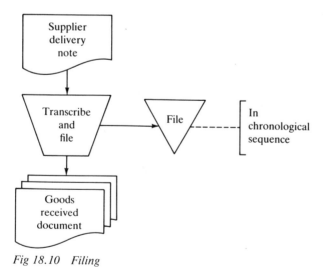

Fig 18.10 Filing

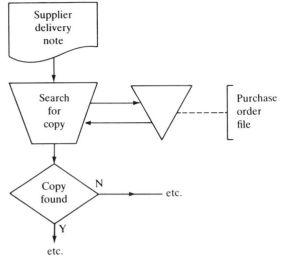

Fig 18.11   Searching a file

Problem
An order is received from a customer. The order is examined and, if it is found to be invalid, the invalid order routine is entered. The customer file is searched and, if a record for the customer cannot be found, the new customer routine is entered.

Where a customer is an existing customer, the order is transcribed onto a two-part internal order form, and the original order filed in customer number sequence. The valid order routine is then entered.

A second problem
Attempt to draw a clerical procedures flowchart which depicts the routine described below. Do not look at the suggested solution (Fig 18.13) until you have attempted the exercise.

When a clerk receives a letter from a customer, it should be determined whether it is a complaint, a notification of a return, or an order. Complaints are passed to the **PR department**, notifications of returns are passed to the **manager**.

An order is then checked and, if any error or query is detected, it is sent to the **section head**.

If the customer placing the order cannot be found in an alphabetically-sequenced customer file, then the order is sent to the **new customer section**.

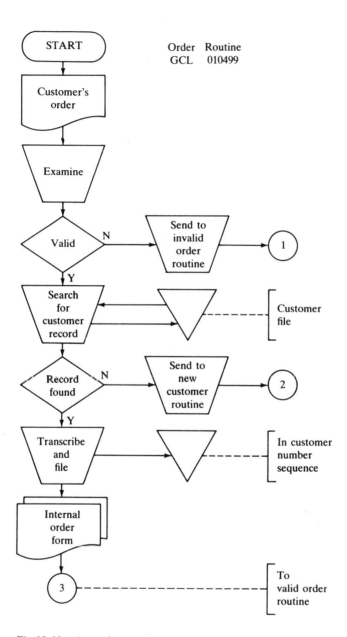

Fig 18.12 An order routine

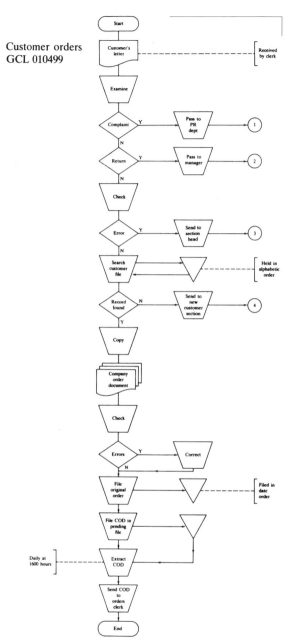

Customer orders
GCL 010499

Fig 18.13 An order routine

A valid order from an existing customer is then copied onto a three-part **company order document**. Any copying errors detected during checking are corrected.

The company order document is placed in a **pending file**, and the original order is filed in date order. At four o'clock each day, the company order documents are sent to the **orders clerk**.

A third problem

In an attempt to clarify the relationships existing in a clerical system, it is common to divide the chart into columns which show the different people or sections involved in an operation.

Consider the following problem: A buying clerk receives a purchase requisition from the storekeeper. (S)he checks it and, if necessary, returns it to the storekeeper for correction.

Using an approved suppliers file, the clerk then attempts to select an appropriate supplier. If this cannot be done, then the requisition is referred to the supervisor, who allocates a supplier, before returning it to the clerk.

A three-part order is then made out. The purchase requisition is filed, and the copies are sent to:

- the supplier
- the storekeeper
- the accounts department

A solution is shown in Fig 18.14.

18.5.8 Data flow diagrams (DFDs)

When the operation of the present system is being investigated, data flow diagrams are often used to show the flow of data through that system and the procedures which take place on it. The diagrams can then be used during the subsequent analysis and design stages.

As is the case with many such charting tools, DFDs can be drawn at various levels of detail. An overall DFD, sometimes known as a **context diagram**, could show a broad outline of the processing, without going into any detail. This could then be supported by more detailed DFDs.

A further point to note is that a DFD can show the **physical** processing of the present system, detailing the departments and individuals concerned in the work, or it can be a **logical DFD** which

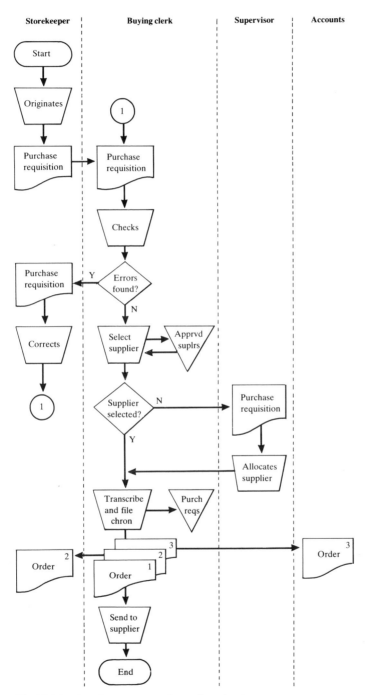

Storekeeper	Buying clerk	Supervisor	Accounts

Start

Originates

Purchase requisition

1

Purchase requisition

Checks

Purchase requisition ← Y — Errors found?

N

Corrects

Select supplier → Apprvd suplrs

1

Supplier selected? — N → Purchase requisition

Y

Allocates supplier

Transcribe and file chron → Purch reqs

Order 2

Order 2

Order 1

Order 3

Send to supplier

End

Fig 18.14   A columnar procedures flowchart

shows *what* happens to the data, rather than *how* the processing is carried out. The use of a logical DFD is often beneficial during the analysis and design stages, as it ignores the present, perhaps manual, way of doing things, thus freeing the systems analyst from the temptation to be over-influenced by the present system. Clerical procedure flowcharts cannot do this.

One last consideration is that, inevitably, various different sets of symbols are used by different people when DFDs are being drawn. This should not prove a problem to the student, however, as the principles remain the same despite such variations.

One set of conventions for drawing DFDs is shown below.

A **source** or **sink** is shown as:

Supplier

A **source** is the point at which data originates outside the processing area which is being charted. A **sink** is the destination for the information which leaves the system. If the drawing of the chart is thereby aided, an entity can be shown more than once on the chart as a source and/or sink.

A **data store** can be shown as follows, with the name of the store entered, along with the number.

| 1 | Invoice file |

A store is a point at which data is held. It thus receives a data flow and/or allows data to be accessed from it. The same store should be shown more than once on the DFD if this helps your charting and the clarity of the finished product.

A **process** can be represented as below:

| 1 | Invoicing |
| Prepare invoice | |

When such notation is used, the nature of the process is entered in the box, along with a number and, optionally, the section or person responsible. A process carries out an activity which converts an incoming data flow into a (different) outgoing data flow.

A **data flow**, known also as a vector, is an arrowed line which shows how data flows around the system, perhaps from one process to another, or from a store to a process, or from a process to a sink:

———————————————➤

A **boundary** is sometimes drawn around a DFD to show (perhaps arbitrarily) the limits of the system which is being charted.

Consider the following example. A purchasing department receives a purchase requisition from the stores. The requisition is checked, and an invalid requisition is returned to the stores for correction. An order is made out using a file of approved suppliers, and sent to the appropriate supplier. A copy order is filed. The requisition is filed.

When the goods are received, the invoice is compared with the filed copy order, and an invalid invoice is returned to the supplier. Valid invoices are passed to the accounts department for payment, and fulfilled orders are filed.

Draw a DFD for the purchase requisition system. Attempt to determine the sources, sinks and files used by this purchase requisition system before reading on.

Our analysis of the problem should lead us to the following points. As we are charting the purchase requisition system, the stores is a source, the accounts department is a sink, and the supplier is both a sink and a source. The files involved are the approved suppliers file, the pending orders file, the requisitions file and the fulfilled orders file. Our chart can then take the form shown in Fig 18.15.

Consider a further example. When an invoice is received from a supplier, it is checked against a file of authorized purchases. If the invoice does not match an authorized purchase, then it is returned to the supplier with a querying letter. If the invoice matches an authorized purchase, but is for an incorrect amount, then it is returned to the supplier with a standard form. If the invoice reconciles, a payment authorization is made out. A cheque is then sent to the supplier, and the invoice and the authorization are filed.

Identify the sources and sinks before proceeding.

The supplier is a source and a sink. The files used are the authorized purchases file, the authorizations file and the invoices file.

Attempt to draw the chart before looking at the suggested solution given in Fig 18.16.

When drawing DFDs, a rough version will almost inevitably need to be drawn as preparation. Identify sources, sinks and files first. A source is often a useful starting place for the drafting. Each time a process takes place, make sure that all the facts necessary for the

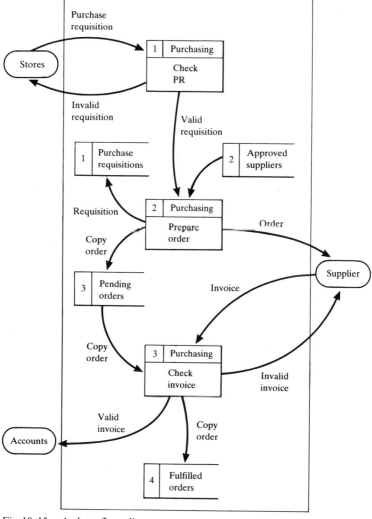

Fig 18.15   A data flow diagram

intended processing are present: the original narrative, after all, may be deficient.

Draw an outline chart first, if this helps to place the system into context. As stated above, repeat sources, sinks and files if required. The chart should then be titled and dated, and the author's name should be added.

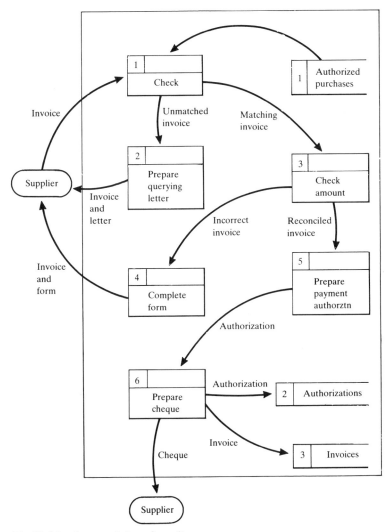

Fig 18.16 A second data flow diagram

18.5.9   Decision tables

Introduction

A decision table is similar to a flowchart in that it is an attempt to replace long-winded and, possibly, confusing narrative with a clear and structured definition of what happens under certain circumstances. There, however, the similarity ends.

We begin our study of decision tables by looking at a simple problem which lends itself to the decision table approach. Students at a college are dealt with according to the following somewhat confusing rules:

1 A student who passes the examinations and completes the coursework and project satisfactorily is awarded a pass.
2 If the coursework and/or the project are not satisfactory, the student is asked to re-submit the unsatisfactory work, as long as the exams have been passed.
3 A student who fails the examinations is deemed to have failed the whole course, unless both the coursework and the project are satisfactory, in which case the student is allowed to re-sit the examinations.

The decision table which depicts this tortuous logic is shown in Fig 18.17. The college's regulations are now shown in a more concise and less confusing form. The three conditions which are relevant to the success or otherwise of a student are shown in the top left-hand quarter of the chart; the five actions which can result are shown in its lower left-hand quarter. The right-hand side of the chart relates a particular student's circumstances, in terms of examination performance, to the actions which will follow. For instance,

Examination regulations GCL 010499								
Exams passed?	Y	Y	Y	Y	N	N	N	N
Course work passed?	Y	Y	N	N	Y	Y	N	N
Project satisfactory?	Y	N	Y	N	Y	N	Y	N
Pass	X							
Fail						X	X	X
Re-do project		X		X				
Re-submit coursework			X	X				
Re-sit examinations					X			

Fig 18.17   A decision table

taking the third column, a student who has

● passed the examinations – Y
● failed the coursework – N
● and passed the project – Y

is asked to re-do the coursework; this is shown by the entry X, for execute, against that action in the third column. A student whose

Decision table	Project:		Program No:
Title:			Table No:
Notes:		By	Date

If	Conditions													

Then	Actions													

Fig 18.18   A decision table form

case is shown in the fifth column has evidently

- failed the examinations − N
- passed the coursework − Y
- and passed the project − Y

and is allowed to re-sit the examinations − as shown by the X.

Constructing a decision table

Let us now see how such a chart could have been built up from the problem in narrative form.

In practice, decision tables are constructed on pre-printed forms such as the one shown in Fig 18.18. Where such forms are not available, then one should be drawn. Thus we start the process of drawing a decision table as follows:

Step 1:   a pre-printed decision table form should be used, or a form should be constructed.
In either case the form's title, the name of the author, and the date should be entered as shown in Fig 18.19.

Step 2:   the conditions which have to be taken into consideration, given the stated problem, are entered into the top left-hand portion of the table.
This is known as the condition stub. Each separate condition should be entered individually; it is best to avoid multiple conditions.

Examination regulations	GCL	010499

Fig 18.19   A decision table form

Step 3: the actions which follow, under different circumstances, from those conditions are next entered.

The actions occupy the lower left-hand portion of the table. This is known as the action stub. Each separate action should be entered individually. At this stage our table would thus take the form shown in Fig 18.20.

Step 4: the number of vertical rules which the table will contain is determined.

A vertical rule is one combination of answers to the questions which have been asked in the condition stub *plus* the indication of the actions which will be carried out in response to that combination of answers. In the table shown in Fig 18.17, for example, there are eight vertical rules; no other combination of answers to the questions asked is possible, given only 'yes' and 'no' answers.

Clearly, the number of combinations of answers, and therefore the number of vertical rules, in a given table depends upon the number of conditions in the condition stub. The number is always 2^c where 'c' represents the number of conditions; in our table, with three conditions, there are thus eight vertical rules.

Step 5: the table's condition entries are completed.

These are in the top right-hand portion of the table, and consist of Ys and Ns. In order to ensure that all combinations of answers to the questions asked in the condition stub are entered, without omission or duplication, the following simple procedure should be adhered to:

1 Entries opposite the lowest condition should be completed, using Y and N alternately, until all the vertical rules have been dealt with.

Examination regulations	GCL	010499
Exams passed? Course work passed? Project satisfactory?		
Pass Fail Re-do project Re-submit coursework Re-sit examinations		

Fig 18.20 Conditions and actions

2 Entries opposite the second-lowest condition should be completed next, using Ys and Ns in pairs alternately, until all rules have been dealt with.

3 Entries for the next condition are then completed using Ys and Ns in fours.

4 This process continues, using twice the number of Ys and Ns each time, until all conditions are completed.

At this point, our table would thus take the form as shown in Fig 18.21.

Step 6:   the action entries in the lower right-hand portion of the table are completed.
This involves completing each vertical rule in turn by entering an X against each action which has to be carried out in that particular set of circumstances. We would place an X against the action 'pass' in the first column of the action entries, as success in each of the three areas of the course (Y,Y,Y) indicates a pass.

We thus arrive at the completed table which we began our discussion by examining (*see* Fig 18.17).

A decision table problem
You should attempt the following decision table exercise before considering the solution.

Orders from new customers are accepted if they are for less than £100; otherwise reference has to be made to the supervisor. Orders from existing customers are accepted.

Consider carefully the following points. Your chart should have two conditions in its condition stub; if a customer is not new then, after all, s/he must be an existing customer! There will thus be four vertical rules.

Examination regulations	GCL		010499					
Exams passed?	Y	Y	Y	Y	N	N	N	N
Course work passed?	Y	Y	N	N	Y	Y	N	N
Project satisfactory?	Y	N	Y	N	Y	N	Y	N
Pass								
Fail								
Re-do project								
Re-submit coursework								
Re-sit examinations								

Fig 18.21   Condition entries

Orders	GCL			010499	
New customer?		Y	Y	N	N
Amount < £100?		Y	N	Y	N
Accept		X		X	X
Refer to supervisor			X		

Fig 18.22   A solution

There are two actions. If your chart does not conform to the above, you should re-draw it before scrutinizing the suggested solution in Fig 18.22. This solution is *not* the only possible one. If your answer differs, carefully check it to ensure that it is correct.

A further problem
You should attempt the following decision table exercise before examining the suggested answer (*see* Fig 18.23).

Candidates are accepted for employment if their qualifications and references are satisfactory, and they pass the interview. Where a candidate's references *or* the interview (but not both) are unsatisfactory, a job for a probationary period is offered. In all other circumstances the candidate's application is rejected.

Your solution may well be different from the one given in Fig 18.23, and yet still be correct. This will be the case if you have entered the conditions or the actions in a different sequence. Check through your answer carefully if you feel this is the case.

Redundancy
Consider the decision table in Fig 18.24, which depicts a (greatly simplified!) procedure for dealing with applicants for motor car insurance.

It should be clear to the reader that the table shown in Fig. 18.24 is not as concise as it could be. The last two vertical rules lead to

Employment selection	GCL		010499						
Qualifications satisfactory?		Y	Y	Y	Y	N	N	N	N
References satisfactory?		Y	Y	N	N	Y	Y	N	N
Passed interview?		Y	N	Y	N	Y	N	Y	N
Accept		X							
Probationary period			X	X					
Reject					X	X	X	X	X

Fig 18.23   A further solution

Insurance GCL	010499			
Age ≥ 25?	Y	Y	N	N
Clean licence?	Y	N	Y	N
Normal terms	X			
Loaded premium		X		
Refuse			X	X

Fig 18.24   A redundant rule

the same action and could therefore be combined into one; this is because, once an applicant is younger than 25 years of age, the application is refused, regardless of the condition of the applicant's licence. The question 'Clean licence?' is redundant, **in the last two rules.**

Redundancy in a decision table is eliminated in the following way.

Step 7:   where two vertical rules have action entries which are exactly the same, and condition entries which differ in one respect only, they can be combined.
This is effected, in the example above, by re-drawing the table as shown in Fig 18.25. As can be seen, the table has been reduced. The two affected vertical rules have been replaced by one rule. The new rule has a **dash** opposite the condition which is irrelevant in those circumstances. In other words, once an applicant is under 25, we show that we are not interested in the state of his/her licence by inserting a dash against the relevant question.

However, it must be noted that some decision tables will not be capable of reduction.

A reduction problem
The decision table shown in Fig. 18.26 is, clearly, one which could be reduced to eliminate redundancy. The reader should attempt to

Insurance GCL	010499		
Age ≥ 25?	Y	Y	N
Clean licence?	Y	N	—
Normal terms	X		
Loaded premium		X	
Refuse			X

Fig 18.25   A reduced table

Discount calculation	GCL			010499				
Existing customer?	Y	Y	Y	Y	N	N	N	N
Cash sale?	Y	Y	N	N	Y	Y	N	N
Amount > £1000?	Y	N	Y	N	Y	N	Y	N
Discount 15%	X							
Discount 10%		X						
Discount 5%			X	X				
No discount					X	X	X	X

Fig 18.26   Calculation of discounts

do this before looking at the suggested solution. Make sure that your reduction goes as far as possible, bearing in mind the rules for reduction which were given above.

The following reductions can be carried out on the table:

- rules 3 and 4 can be combined to form a new rule 3
- rules 5 and 6 can be combined to form a new rule 4
- rules 7 and 8 can be combined to form a new rule 5
- the new rules 4 and 5 can themselves be combined

If your solution does not take account of these points, you should attempt the problem again before looking at the solution shown in Fig 18.27. This table cannot be reduced any further, as no two vertical rules satisfy the criteria for reduction which we have laid down. We can carry out a rudimentary check on our reduction by:

- counting each vertical rule without any dashes in it as one rule; such a rule is, after all, the same rule as the original table contained
- counting each vertical rule with one dash in it as two because two vertical rules have been combined into one in such a case

Discount calculation	GCL		010499	
Existing customer?	Y	Y	Y	N
Cash sale?	Y	Y	N	—
Amount > £1000?	Y	N	—	—
Discount 15%	X			
Discount 10%		X		
Discount 5%			X	
No discount				X

Fig 18.27   The reduced table

- counting rules with two dashes in them as four original rules, and so on. The formula in each case is $R = 2^D$ where D is the number of dashes in a vertical rule in a reduced table, and R is the number of rules in the original table which a reduced rule represents

In the example above, then:

$$1 + 1 + 2 + 4 = 8 = 2^3 = 2^c$$

where C is the number of conditions in the table

Step 8: reduction should be checked

A second problem involving redundancy
Draw up a decision table which embodies the following rules. To be eligible for early retirement, an applicant must:

- be earning over £10,000
- be on grade 3 or above
- be monthly paid
- in the case of a man, be aged 55 or over
- in the case of a woman, have at least five years' service

Clearly, as there are several conditions in the question, then the full table will be a fairly large one. In order to avoid the clerical effort involved in drawing up such a table, the reader is recommended to attempt to draw the reduced table straightaway.

Hint . . . if an employee is *not* earning more than £10 000, then (s)he *cannot* retire early!

Try to find a solution yourself before examining the solution in Fig 18.28. The reader should have determined that the above

Early retirement	GCL				010499		
Earning over £10,000?	Y	Y	Y	Y	Y	Y	N
On grade 3 at least?	Y	Y	Y	Y	Y	N	—
Monthly-paid?	Y	Y	Y	Y	N	—	—
Male?	Y	Y	N	N	—	—	—
Aged 55 or over?	Y	N	—	—	—	—	—
At least 5 years service?	—	—	Y	N	—	—	—
Eligible	X		X				
Not eligible		X		X	X	X	X

$2 + 2 + 2 + 2 + 8 + 16 + 32 = 64 = 2^6 = 2^c$

Fig 18.28

problem requires the following six conditions:

1 Salary > £10 000
2 Grade > or = 3
3 Monthly-paid
4 Sex = Male
5 Age > or = 55
6 Service > or = 5

Also notice that an N in answer to any of the first three questions will result in the rejection of the application.

A last consideration is that the question concerning age is only applicable to men, while the question concerning service is only relevant to women.

If your solution does not take account of these points, then you should make a further attempt to draw up the table before looking at a suggested answer (Fig 18.28).

Impossible rules
In the examples which we have looked at so far, all the conditions are independent of each other; it is possible, for example, for an employee to be on Grade 2 or Grade 9 regardless of the number of years' service, and it is possible for employees to be earning £9 000 or £11 000 regardless of whether they are 54 or 56 years of age. This means that, for such problems, **all combinations** of Y and N are valid, because all combinations could exist in the 'real world'.

This will *not* be the case, however, when the questions in a decision table are related to each other. Consider an example: bonuses are calculated according to the following rules: employees with less than three years' service receive no bonus; male employees with three or more years' service who are at least 60 years old receive five per cent bonus; other male employees with three or more years' service receive three per cent bonus. The same rules apply to women, but the relevant age is 55.

Attempt to draw the full decision table in respect of the above problem before considering the solution shown in Fig 18.29.

Clearly, vertical rules 2, 6, 10 and 14 are impossible, as a person cannot be over 60 and not be over 55. If a full decision table is called for in an examination, and there are impossible rules in it, then, as was done in Fig 18.29, the action entries for the impossible rules should be left blank. An explanatory note should also be appended to the table.

Bonus calculation GCL 010499															
Less than 3 years' service	Y	Y	Y	Y	Y	Y	Y	Y	N	N	N	N	N	N	N	N
Male	Y	Y	Y	Y	N	N	N	N	Y	Y	Y	Y	N	N	N	N
At least 60 years old	Y	Y	N	N	Y	Y	N	N	Y	Y	N	N	Y	Y	N	N
At least 55 years old	Y	N	Y	N	Y	N	Y	N	Y	N	Y	N	Y	N	Y	N
No bonus	X		X	X	X		X	X								
3% bonus											X	X				X
5% bonus									X				X		X	

Note: rules 2, 6, 10 and 14 are impossible.

Fig 18.29   Impossible rules

When a decision table with impossible rules in it is reduced to eliminate redundancy, then hyphens can be used to cover impossibility as in Fig 18.30.

As usual, redundancy, whether due to indifference or impossibility, should be checked and the checking should be shown.

Linked tables

Where it is felt that a problem will result in an unwieldy table, then it is possible to split that table into two or more **linked** or **nested** tables. The problem considered in the previous section could then be answered as shown in Fig 18.31.

Reduction can be checked by multiplying the number of rules in each table together:

$$4 \times 2 \times 2 = 16 = 2^4 = 2^c$$

The else rule

Under certain circumstances, even after reduction has been effected, it will be the case that a decision table constructed

Bonus calculation GCL 010499					
Less than 3 years' service?	Y	N	N	N	N
Male?	—	Y	Y	N	N
At least 60 years old?	—	Y	Y	N	—
At least 55 years old?	—	—	—	Y	N
No bonus	X				
3% bonus			X		X
5% bonus		X		X	

$8 + 2 + 2 + 2 + 2 = 16 = 2^4 = 2^c$.

Fig 18.30   The reduced table

Table 1	GCL		010499	
Service < 3 years?	Y	N	N
Male?	—	Y	N
No bonus	X		
Go to table 2		X	
Go to table 3			X

Table 2	GCL	010499	
Age at least 60	Y	N
3% bonus		X
5% bonus	X	

Table 3	GCL	010499	
Age at least 55	Y	N
3% bonus		X
5% bonus	X	

Fig 18.31   Nested tables

according to the conventions laid down before appears clumsily long-winded. Consider the case proposed in Fig 18.32.

As there are five conditions relevant to our treatment of a job applicant, the full table will have 32 vertical rules, and yet we are really only interested in two of them! Even after reduction there are still six rules.

A neater way to depict the required logic in such a case is to use the **else rule**. The use of the rule in this case would produce the table shown in Fig 18.33.

Clearly, the use of the else rule produces a more succinct table,

Selection	GCL		010499				
Qualifications satisfactory?	Y	Y	Y	Y	Y	N
Adequate experience?	Y	Y	Y	Y	N	—
Interview satisfactory?	Y	Y	Y	N	—	—
References acceptable?	Y	Y	N	—	—	—
Passed aptitude test?	Y	N	—	—	—	—
Offer programming job	X					
Refer to personnel manager		X				
Reject			X	X	X	X

Fig 18.32   A large table

Selection	GCL	010499			
					Else
Qualifications satisfactory?			Y	Y	
Adequate experience?			Y	Y	
Interview satisfactory?			Y	Y	
References acceptable?			Y	Y	
Passed aptitude test?			Y	N	
Offer programming job			X		
Refer to personnel manager				X	
Reject					X

Fig 18.33   The else rule

and the critical rules in any given situation are highlighted. And yet the advantage of being able to check the final table, as we did after reduction above, is lost.

It is recommended that, in an examination, you only use the 'else rule' if you are specifically asked so to do.

Extended-entry tables
The decision tables which we have been dealing with so far in this section are known as **limited-entry decision tables**. This is because the entries which we are permitted to make are limited to Y's, N's, dashes and X's.

Clearly, rigid adherence to this format will sometimes produce unsatisfactory results. Consider the table shown in Fig 18.34.

As all the conditions are interrelated, and as only one action can be carried out in any one vertical rule, the table takes on an odd shape. This problem can be overcome by using an **extended-entry table**, as shown in Fig 18.35. As can be seen in an extended-entry table, entries other than Y, N dash and X can be used. Clearly, a

Insurance	GCL	010499			
Age < 21?			Y	N	N	N
Age < 25?			—	Y	N	N
Age < 30?			—	—	Y	N
No discount			X			
Discount 10%				X		
Discount 25%					X	
Discount 33%						X

Fig 18.34   A limited-entry table

	Insurance	GCL	010499		
Age?		<21	<25	<30	⩾30
Discount %		0	10	25	33

Fig 18.35   An extended-entry table

hybrid decision table which uses a combination of Y's, N's, dashes and other entries in the condition entries, and a combination of X's and other entries in the action entries, may be used. A hybrid table is shown in Fig 18.36.

It is probably safer not to use extended entries in an examination, unless you are asked to.

Points to consider
Decision tables may be used in computer work whenever they are an appropriate and convenient method of expressing processing logic. When deciding, in a given situation, whether to use decision tables or to represent requirements in some other way, the computer practitioner would be aware of the following considerations:

1   While many different sets of conventions exist for flowcharts, decision tables are virtually standardized. This means that, after a brief explanation, a novice can understand easily what a table is trying to say; the communication process is thus aided.

2   Communication is further aided by the fact that the conditions are clearly separated from the actions.

3   When a pre-printed decision table form is used, tables are easy and quick to draw, lending themselves to typing; no special equipment such as a flowchart template is required, and no special training need be given. It could be further argued that, unlike flowcharting, which needs a special aptitude for its efficient execution, the drawing-up of decision tables is a fairly mechanical task which

	Insurance	GCL	010499		
Clean licence? Age?		Y <18	Y <21	Y <25	Y ⩾25	N —
Accept Reject Discount %		X	X 0	X 10	X 20	 X

Fig 18.36   A hybrid table

can be handled by almost anyone; many computer personnel, however, would not agree with this.

4   When only a few conditions and a few actions are involved, a table may be a clear and concise way of expressing the logic which relates them. Tables, however, become unwieldy when more than five or six conditions are necessary. This can often be overcome, as we have seen, by splitting the problem up into several sections, and devoting a table to each section. The tables can then be linked together by an action such as: **Go to table 3**.

Of course, an action can also cause the processing to loop back to the start of the same table, if required.

When smaller tables are used and thus linked, amendments become easier to handle, although many practitioners argue that charts show the flow of operations more clearly.

5   It is argued that flowcharts are solution-oriented, in that they show *how* a problem should be solved, giving the sequence of tests and actions. Decision tables, on the other hand, can be said to be problem-oriented; they show only *what* is required.

6   We saw in Chapter 16 that standard software is available which translates decision tables into program statements, prior to compilation. This being the case, the sequence of events when a system is being developed could take the following pattern:

- the analyst and the user agree the processing logic required; this is documented in DT form and becomes part of the system specification
- the analyst includes the same DT in the appropriate program specification
- the programmer incorporates the table into the program, and it is handled automatically by the decision table pre-processor

In effect, the user's definition of the required processing has gone directly into the machine, without the intervention of a third party!

7   Limited-entry decision tables which do not use the else rule can be checked for completeness. This forces the person completing the table to ensure that no loose ends are left. No such systematic check can be carried out on a flowchart.

Points to note
In practice, the person creating a decision table chooses whether to use a limited-entry table or a table with extended entries, s/he decides whether or not to reduce the table, and either uses or does

not use the else rule. In an examination, if the requirements are not precisely stated, a full limited-entry table should first be drawn and, as a separate exercise, the table should then be re-drawn in its reduced form. Only if specially asked for should extended entries or the else rule be used.

18.6 Analysis of recorded facts

Once facts concerning the present system have been found and recorded, it is necessary for the systems analyst to analyse them, so that the task of designing a new system can be tackled.

The aims of the analyst during this stage are thus:

1 To examine carefully the existing system, making sure that the weaknesses, duplications, omissions and redundant elements in it are identified. This will allow the analyst to ensure that the new system will eliminate such deficiencies, simplify processes where possible and include any further processing which is needed.
2 To identify the data and information which is an essential part of the system, so that the new system will be able to cater for it.
3 To produce a statement of requirements for the approval of the user.

During the analysis stage, the analyst carefully scrutinizes the recorded facts, perhaps using tables on which fields are related to the forms upon which they appear, or charts which show the flow of forms and other documents through the system. In these and other ways, the analyst will be taking a look at the recorded facts from a new angle, and new implications will come to light. This will help to achieve the aims stated above.

A document which the system analyst can use to help the analysis of the recorded facts is the **grid chart**, often known as the **X-chart**. This form allows data items to be cross-referenced, in an attempt to bring to light relationships which would otherwise perhaps not be apparent.

A completed example is shown in Fig 18.37.

Perusal of the completed form shows that none of the specified outputs uses the field 'industry code'. This may not have been apparent to the analyst previously, and might well need further investigation – *what* is the code used for?

In a similar way, fields can be analysed by department of use (*see* Fig 18.38). Such a completed form might indicate that some

Form				
Field	Invoice	Statement	Sales statistics	Total
Customer name	X	X		2
Customer reference	X	X	X	3
Address	X	X		2
Region code			X	1
Industry code				0

Fig 18.37   A grid chart

Department				
Field	Stores	Marketing	Accounts	Total
Part number	X	X	X	3
Description	X	X	X	3
Quantity	X	X	X	3

Fig 18.38   A further grid chart

'streamlining' of documents could be called for, as all the affected departments seem to use the specified fields.

18.7   The statement of requirements

As a result of the analysis of recorded facts, the systems analyst will know *what* the new system is going to have to do, although s/he will not yet know *how* it is going to do it. It is a sound precaution to obtain the user's approval of the analyst's work at this stage, before any further work is undertaken.

A formal **statement of requirements** is thus usually produced by the analyst before systems design is begun. Any contentious points in this document can thus be cleared up 'on the spot'; at least the analyst knows that the user's thinking is in line with his/her own in general terms, before detailed design of the new system commences.

18.8   Summary

Before a systems analyst can design a new computer system, a thorough investigation has to be carried out. This involves fact finding and fact recording, followed by a careful analysis of what has been discovered. At the end of the systems investigation phase, the analyst documents the findings in a formal statement of requirements; only when this has been approved by the prospective 'user' of the computer system, can design work begin.

Questions

Note that answers to selected questions appear in the Appendix at the end of the volume.

True or false?

1 An initial assignment brief acts as a terms of reference for the systems analyst carrying out the project feasibility study.

2 The main aim of a project feasibility study is to determine whether or not it is possible to carry out a given task using the computer.

3 A project feasibility report is mainly concerned with recommending new computer hardware.

4 A systems analyst should always start the investigation stage by sending out questionnaires.

5 Questionnaires are most useful where a small number of respondents are concerned.

6 Interviewing is the most common form of fact finding employed by systems analysts.

7 A clerical procedures flowchart is used to depict processing steps which are carried out manually.

8 Using a decision table pre-processor, a DT can be, in effect, fed directly into the computer.

Multiple choice (circle one letter in each)

9 Before an analyst begins to carry out a project feasibility study, (s)he is given a formal document. This is known as:
  (a) a terms of reference
  (b) a project brief
  (c) an initial assignment brief
  (d) all of the above
  (e) none of the above

10 A project feasibility study:
  (a) helps the analyst to determine whether or not a particular task is possible on the computer

(b)   is carried out in conjunction with computer manufacturers in order to determine whether a computer should be acquired

(c)   helps the analyst to determine whether a particular task is worth computerizing

(d)   should be carried out after a new system has been implemented

(e)   must always be carried out by the analyst who is going to design the new system

11   Systems investigation includes:

(a)   fact finding

(b)   fact recording

(c)   analysis of recorded facts

(d)   all of the above

(e)   (b) + (c)

12   How many vertical rules will there be in a full, limited entry, decision table which has four conditions and three actions?

(a)   16 (2^4)

(b)   12 (3×4)

(c)   8 (4×2)

(d)   9 (3^2)

(e)   8 (2^3)

Examination questions

1   Outline and comment on the objectives and various stages of a feasibility study for a proposed business system. You are to assume a medium-sized organization that already has sufficient computing power to cover its foreseeable needs.

(Chartered Association of Certified Accountants)

2   Identify, describe and briefly evaluate the techniques of fact finding and fact recording available to both the systems analyst and an O & M officer when investigating a system within an organization.

(Chartered Association of Certified Accountants)

3   Explain how a systems analyst investigates a business system.

(Chartered Association of Certified Accountants)

4   Fact finding is an importan: part of the systems analysis process.

(a)   Explain why fact finding is important

(b)   List the principal methods of obtaining facts, describing the advantages and disadvantages of each method.

(Institute of Cost and Management Accountants)

5   Assume that you are employed as a systems analyst by a large company which has recently, and after some resistance, taken over a much smaller company, XY Ltd, which manufactures similar

products. It is company policy to make the smaller firm's systems uniform with its own, which are computer-based. As a first step it is intended to investigate sales ledger procedures at XY Ltd and you are in charge of the investigation.

(a) What do you expect to be the biggest problem which you will face?

(b) Make an orderly and logical check list of the main topics that you intend to cover in your fact-finding interviews with the sales accounting staff at XY Ltd.

(Chartered Association of Certified Accountants)

6 You are a systems analyst working on a project for the transfer of sales ledger procedures to computer operation.

(a) Prepare a detailed and orderly checklist of the main points you would cover in your fact-finding interviews with sales accounting staff.

(b) In your new system, the sales accounting staff are able to call up a customer's account on to the screen of a VDU. List ten data items you would expect to be displayed on the screen.

(Chartered Association of Certified Accountants)

7 (a) State the main guidelines a systems analyst should follow when conducting a fact-finding interview.

(b) An analyst will usually complete a document description form for each of the forms used in the system under investigation. Sketch a neat draft of your design of such a form. Sample entries are not required.

(Chartered Association of Certified Accountants)

8 Draft a procedure flowchart of the following account of the routine for preparing purchase orders in XYZ Ltd.

Purchase request forms from the various departments are received daily by the purchase department. The assistant buyer divides the forms into three categories; raw material, consumables and services. The consumables and services forms are passed to the section leader for action. In the case of requests for raw material, the assistant buyer refers to a register which lists the main suppliers for each type of raw material, the total orders placed already against these suppliers and whether or not contracts have been negotiated with a particular supplier. In the light of this information, the assistant buyer then assigns a supplier to each purchase request form, writing the name and number of the supplier on the form. When the order forms part of a current contract, the contract code number is also entered. The assistant buyer then passes the forms to the prices clerk who, by reference to the suppliers' price lists, enters prices on the form and calculates the value of the order. When returned to the assistant buyer, the forms are accumulated in an 'awaiting typing' file. Twice weekly the accumulated purchase requests are passed to the typing pool for the origination of six-part purchase orders.

Typed purchase orders are checked against the original requests, and orders requiring amendment or re-typing are returned to the typing section. Purchase orders which pass checking are then passed to the buyer for signature.

(Chartered Association of Certified Accountants)

9 The following is a description of the clerical procedures for the receipt of goods in a stores department. You are required to draw a flowchart of the procedures.

When goods are received by the stores department, the storeman takes the delivery note from the goods and searches his 'awaiting delivery' file for the stores copy of the purchase order. (If he cannot find it he reports to the supervisor.) When he has found it, he checks that the goods received, as shown on the delivery note, agree with the items and quantities shown on the stores copy of the purchase order. He refers any queries to the supervisor. He enters the date received on the purchase order, staples it to the delivery note, and then files both documents in purchase order number sequence in an 'awaiting GRS' file. Twice weekly (on Mondays and Fridays) he takes all the documents from the 'awaiting GRS' file and uses them to prepare a three-part goods received sheet set. Top copies, together with relevant purchase order copies and delivery notes, are sent to the purchasing department for accounts payable routine; second copies go to the supervisor, third copies are retained in a 'GRS completed' file.

(Chartered Association of Certified Accountants)

10 You are required to draw a flowchart of the system described below.

The order handling department of a pharmaceutical company receives all customers' orders. Standard stock items are dealt with by a standardized procedure while special order items are passed to the production control department.

Stock items are priced and the discount category ascertained. After pricing, the customer's credit limit is checked and if the limit is exceeded the order is referred to the accounts department. If the items are temporarily out-of-stock the order is held on a 'back order' file in the order handling department. If the stock and credit positions are satisfactory a six-part invoice is prepared. Copies 1, 2 and 3, which will go eventually to the customer, accounts department and sales order file respectively, are detached and placed in a pending file to await notification of despatch. Copies 4, 5 and 6, which are respectively advice note, packing note and despatch copy, are sent to the warehouse for processing.

(Institute of Cost and Management Accountants)

11 The following is a description for dealing with delivery charges for goods bought from AB Ltd.

For the purpose of determining delivery charges, customers are divided into two categories, those whose sales region code (SRC) is 50 or above, and those with an SRC of less than 50.

If the SRC is less than 50 and the invoice amount is less than £1000, the delivery charge to be added to the invoice total is £30. But if the invoice value is for £1000 or more, the delivery charge is £15.

If the SRC is equal to or greater than 50 and the invoice total is less than £1000, the delivery charge is £40. For invoices totalling £1000 or more, however, the delivery charge is £20.

Required:
(a) Prepare a decision table of the above procedure.
(b) Prepare a flowchart of the above procedure.
(c) List briefly *four* advantages claimed for decision tables over flowcharts.   (Chartered Association of Certified Accountants)

12 Construct decision tables (a) without the use of the 'dash-rule' and (b) with the use of the 'dash-rule' which reflect the logic shown in the flowchart segment shown in Fig 18.39.

13 An insurance company invites applications from motorists regarding insurance cover. Applicants are required to submit the following details:

● name and address
● age
● number of accidents in the last ten years
● licence type – provisional or full

The rules regarding acceptance are as follows:

● motorists who are 31 or over, with no accidents in the last ten years, who hold a full licence, are accepted for full cover
● motorists who are 31 or over, with no accidents in the last ten

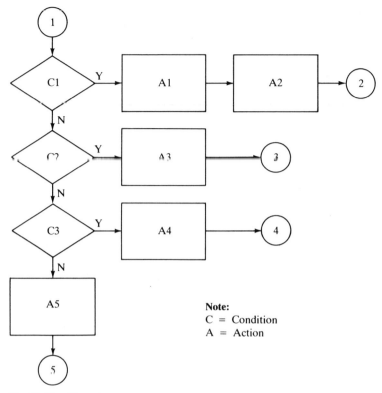

Fig 18.39   Flowchart segment

years, who hold a provisional licence, are accepted for third-
party cover
● all others are rejected

(a) Draw up, in full, a limited-entry decision table which covers
the above rules.

(b) Without using the else rule, reduce your table to eliminate
redundancies therein.

14 A company allows discounts according to the following rules;

● new customers are allowed no discounts
● existing customers are allowed ten per cent discount, and a
   further five per cent discount if their outstanding balance is less
   than £200 and if the value of their order is more than £100.

(a) Draw a full, limited-entry, decision table in respect of the
above rules.

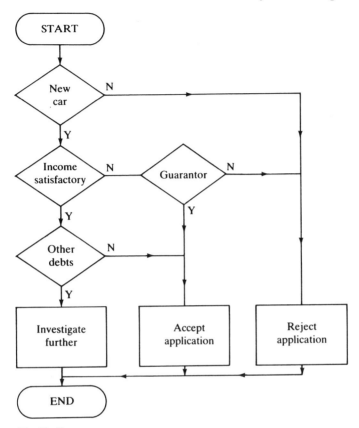

Fig 18.40

(b) Draw a reduced limited-entry table, using the 'dash' rule.

15 A finance company applies the following rules when dealing with applications for loans for the purchase of motor vehicles (see Fig 18.40).

(a) Draw a full, limited-entry, decision table for the rules.

(b) Reduce the table using dashes, but without using 'else'.

16 Assuming that you are a project leader conducting a systems study covering all commercial activities in a company, who would you include in your study team and why? State the industry for which your selection would be suitable.

Summarize: (a) the main steps and (b) the work involved in such a systems study.

(Institute of Cost and Management Accountants)

19

Systems design

19.1 Introduction

19.1.1 The objectives

Once the systems analyst has carried out an investigation of an existing system, and has produced a statement of requirements which has been approved by the user, the systems design stage can begin. At this point the analyst is bringing together his or her computer expertise and the knowledge gained of the business systems under review, in order to design an efficient computerized system. In short, the objectives are to design a system which:

1 meets the user's needs as cost-effectively as possible, bearing in mind that this system is only in effect one sub-system within the whole organization's scheme of things;
2 is within the constraints laid down in the analyst's terms of reference, as well as any legal or other constraints which may affect it;
3 processes data accurately, and is sufficiently robust to withstand fraudulent attempts to abuse it;
4 is simple in its operation;
5 has sufficient flexibility built into it to ensure that its maintenance and its development over time will be easily and cheaply

accomplished. Many organizations, after all, see growth as a prime aim.

19.1.2   One approach

In what follows we shall, of course, simplify greatly the task of systems design. In particular it will be presented, for ease of understanding, as a series of consecutive steps. But systems design, like any design process, is not in fact like that. In practice, an analyst probably works in cycles, working at increasingly detailed levels, going back and making changes as required, until a completely satisfactory design is arrived at. These points should be borne in mind throughout this chapter, in which we shall deal with systems design under the following seven headings:

- the nature of the system
- its output
- the files which are maintained
- the system's input
- the processing tasks required
- systems flowcharts
- control over accuracy

19.2   The nature of the system

Before detailed work can be started on the design of the files maintained by a computer system, or the output produced by that system, the analyst has to make a major decision about the nature of the system. In effect, a decision has to be taken whether the system will be:

1   one which is run periodically, say weekly or monthly. When using such a system, all the transactions relating to the period concerned are assembled into a batch, and applied to the relevant master file(s) in one run. Clearly, such a system will produce periodic reports. A payroll system is an example of such a **batch processing** system. Batch systems, because of their cyclic nature, are also known as **time-driven** systems.
2   one which allows enquiries and transactions to be applied to the master file(s) as and when required, and which gives the user instant information as a result of such happenings. Such a system is called a **real-time** system, and we saw an example of real-time processing

in Chapter 4 when we looked at a banking system. An alternative name for real-time systems is **event-driven** or **transaction-driven** systems.
3   or one which will be a combination of, or a variation upon, these two.

Clearly, only when the unique circumstances relating to a particular system are known, can its nature be determined.

19.3   Output design

19.3.1   Points to be considered

The design of the output which is going to be produced by a computer system is a logical point to begin the process of detailed systems design. After all, there is little point in postponing the task of designing the output, only to find that the files which have been carefully specified do not allow a particular item of information to be produced!

When embarking upon the phase of systems design, the systems analyst will already know the responsibilities of a particular manager, section or department. Therefore the information necessary to enable those responsibilities to be efficiently carried out can then be produced. In particular, the analyst must make decisions about the following points:

1   In a real-time system, much information will be produced on demand, but other reports, periodic in nature, may also be required. In a batch system, of course, all the reports will be periodic. In either case the **frequency** of reporting, and the **timing** of such reports, will have to be carefully thought out, and a balance will have to be struck between the extra benefits, if any, derived from more frequent reports, and the increased costs thereby incurred.
2   The **contents** of a report will need to be determined. This will involve deciding which fields of information are really **needed** in a report, and deciding upon the **volume** of output which a particular application warrants. Of course, the principle of **exception reporting**, where only items which are unexpectedly high or low are reported upon, should be used wherever it is appropriate.
3   The **sequence** of items in a report is often crucial. Payslips produced purely in employee number sequence, for example, may be

difficult to distribute in a large factory; a better approach may be to produce them in number sequence *within* department code.

4 The **medium** and **device** to be used for a particular piece of output will have to be carefully chosen. As we saw in Chapter 5, the printer may not be the only answer, and the use of microfilm or visual display units are just two alternatives which may well repay consideration. Speed of response may well be an important criterion here.

Above all, the systems designer should remember the objectives set, i.e. the attempt to design a system which will economically aid human beings who have certain tasks to carry out. The benefits derived from the production of information by a system should always outweigh the costs of producing that information.

19.3.2 Approval of output

The output which a system is going to produce will have to be carefully defined in the document in which the analyst proposes the new system – the systems specification. If printed output is to be used, as it often will be, sample reports can be included on special squared paper known as **print layout forms**; this will enable the user to see what the information is going to look like. Better still, a general-purpose print program could be used to actually produce a sample report on the printer. Where a visual display unit is to be proposed as a method of outputting information from a system, a special program could be written to cause a sample report to be displayed on such a device, thus giving the users a chance to see exactly what their staff are being asked to deal with. Once again, however, costs will have to be carefully considered.

It will be helpful if such samples can be shown to the user as soon as the output has been designed, rather than later when the systems specification is produced. Much time and effort may well be saved if errors and omissions can be spotted at an early stage.

19.4 File design

19.4.1 Hit-rate

When we discussed backing storage media in Chapter 6, we encountered the concept of the **hit-rate**. A master file's hit-rate is the percentage of its records which need to be accessed in one run.

Clearly, this concept will have a great bearing upon the file design opted for in a given set of circumstances.

19.4.2   File design in a real-time system

Let us first consider some of the points which an analyst would have to sort out when designing files for use in a real-time system.

As enquiries and transactions can be input to the system at random, we are dealing with one-off processing. This is, in effect, a special case of low hit-rate processing and we therefore would need to hold the file in a form which facilitates **direct access processing**. We could employ a type of **random organization** similar to that we looked at in a simplified form in Chapter 6. This, of course, could not be accomplished with a magnetic tape file, because of the serial nature of tape, and so a disk file would be needed. It should be clear that these considerations still apply even if more than one file is needed by a system.

Notice how we have attempted to reduce the file design process to a series of logical steps (*see* Fig 19.1).

19.4.3   File design in a batch system

Unfortunately, file design becomes a more complex issue, even at this much simplified level, when we move on to batch systems.

Let us begin, however, with a simple case. Suppose we are considering the design of a master file for a payroll system. The system

Q. What is the hit-rate?
A. Very low (one-off).

Q. What file organization is appropriate?
A. Random organization.

Q. What medium is appropriate?
A. Magnetic disk.

Fig 19.1   The file design process

is a batch system with a high hit-rate, as most records, if not all of them, will be accessed during a run. This leads to the belief that a sequential file organization would be the most efficient, as little or no time would then be lost accessing inactive records during a run. A sequential master file can, of course, be held on either tape or disk. But we saw in Chapter 6 that tapes are too slow and inflexible for today's large modern computers; disk would therefore be used. Once again, note that we have attempted to reduce the file design to a series of logical steps (*see* Fig 19.2).

However, the hit-rate of a master file used in a batch processing system need not necessarily be high. Take the case of a file which records details of the stock items held in a company's warehouse – let us assume that one million different items are in stock. If it is required to update the file weekly and produce a report for each part which has been active during the week, and if only 5000 items are sold each week, then the file will have a low hit-rate. Clearly, random access would be far more efficient in such a case than would sequential access, with hundreds of thousands of records needlessly hit. Once again, our approach is shown in Fig 19.3.

A further problem relating to batch processing systems concerns a master file which has, at different times, both a high hit-rate and a low hit-rate.

Consider the following. A system sends invoices every day to those customers who have been active; relatively few customers are active each day. Every month, statements are sent to customers who have been active during the month; most customers are active during any given month.

Q. What is the hit-rate?
A. High.

Q. What file organization is appropriate?
A. Sequential organization.

Q. What medium is appropriate?
A. Tape or disk.

Fig 19.2   A high hit-rate file

Q. What is the hit-rate?
A. Low.

Q. What file organization is appropriate?
A. Random organization.

Q. What medium is appropriate?
A. Disk.

Fig 19.3 A low hit-rate batch system

Only one master file is involved but at different times it has different hit-rates! Let us attempt to use our previous approach (*see* Fig 19.4).

A further complication involves a hybrid system which is *both* a real-time *and* a batch system.

Consider the following problem. A payroll/personnel system pays employees weekly. It also allows enquiries to be made of the master file as and when required.

Let us examine the problem (Fig 19.5).

It should be carefully noted at this stage, then, that batch processing does not necessarily imply the use of sequential processing;

Q. What is the hit-rate?
A. Both high and low.

Q. What file organization is appropriate?
A. Indexed-sequential.

Q. What medium is appropriate?
A. Disk.

Fig 19.4 High and low hit-rates

Q. What is the hit-rate?
A. Both high and low.

Q. What file organization is appropriate?
A. Indexed-sequential.

Q. What medium is appropriate?
A. Disk.

Fig 19.5   A hybrid system

nor does the use of sequential processing necessarily imply the use of magnetic tape. What we have said so far can be summarized in Fig 19.6.

19.4.4 Multi-file systems

Many systems, in practice, will need to update more than one master file to function effectively; an invoicing system, for example, would need to update a stock file and a customer file. The

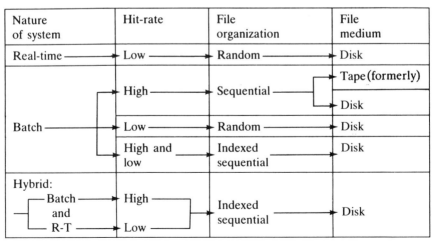

Nature of system	Hit-rate	File organization	File medium
Real-time	Low	Random	Disk
Batch	High	Sequential	Tape (formerly) / Disk
	Low	Random	Disk
	High and low	Indexed sequential	Disk
Hybrid: Batch and R-T	High / Low	Indexed sequential	Disk

Fig 19.6   File design

points made above still apply, but thought will also need to be given to the interaction of the two files. We shall discuss systems which need more than one master file later in this chapter when we examine systems flowcharts.

19.5   Input design

19.5.1   Points to be considered

Having established the output required from a system and the files which will need to be held in order to help produce that output, the analyst can deal with the design of the system's input. The input must be capable of:

● keeping the master file(s) up to date; and
● producing, in conjunction with data from the file(s), the required output

At this stage, the analyst must make decisions about the following points:

1 In a real-time system, enquiries and transactions will be input as and when required. In a batch system, however, input will need to be catered for on a cyclic basis. Thus, the **frequency** of the input and its **timing** will have to be carefully thought out, usually in conjunction with the frequency and timing of the output.

2 The **contents** of the records which are to be input to the system will need to be determined, as an item which is later to appear in the output will need, unless it is generated by a program, to come from a master record or from an input record. This leads on directly to considerations of **volume**; how can the amount of input be reduced?

3 The **medium** and **device** to be used for a particular piece of input will have to be carefully chosen. As we saw in Chapter 4, many different methods of input are available, and the analyst, in a given set of circumstances, will have to choose the optimum one. The speed of response which is required will be an important consideration here.

19.5.2   Code design

When inputting data to a computer system, and when holding that data on a master file within the system, it would be slow and costly to use the narrative descriptions which human beings are accustomed to use in their everyday work. For this reason, codes are used so that different items can be represented with economy of definition.

Sometimes, when an analyst is designing a new system, little choice is given as to the type of code to use, because the cost and disruption which would ensue from a changeover from the existing code would rule out such a change. At other times, however, the analyst will be in a position to design a new coding system for the items with which the new system is going to deal. In such circumstances, a knowledge of the different types of code which are in common use would be of assistance.

Several different coding systems exist, many of them being subtle variations on each other. We consider a few of the major ones below.

1 Sequence codes, also known as **progressive codes**, entail the allocation of numbers to items in straightforward numerical sequence; there is no obvious connection between an item and its code. For example:

00001	**steel screws**
00002	**brass washers**
00003	**steel bolts**

2 Group classification codes are an improvement on the simple codes described above. In such a code, a digit, often the first digit, indicates the classification into which a particular item falls. For example:

1nnnn	**could be a screw**
2nnnn	**could be a washer**

and so on. In effect, a pre-fix signifies the group to which the item belongs, so that items would be together if the records relative to the items were held in sequential order.

Improvements can be made on this; three are discussed below.

3 Faceted codes give more information about an item, because each digit, or perhaps a pair of digits, represents some facet or characteristic of the item. For example:

- the first digit could represent the nature of the product:
  1 = screws
  2 = nuts
  3 = bolts
  etc.
- the second digit could represent the material from which the item is made:
  1 = steel
  2 = brass
  3 = copper
  etc.
- the third digit could give the size:
  1 = one inch
  2 = half inch
  etc.

An item whose code is 121nn is thus a one inch brass screw.

4 A significant digit code takes this idea one step further by representing a feature of the item by digits which directly relate to it. In the examples below, for instance, the second to fifth digits could represent a vehicle's engine size:

n0845nn = a car with an 845 c.c. engine;
n1500nn = a car with a 1500 c.c. engine, etc.

5 A decimal or **hierarchical code** is a type of faceted code where each digit represents a classification, digits further to the right representing a smaller sub-set than the ones to the left, and where decimal points are used to break up the code number into its main constituent parts. Thus a library could classify its books as follows:

1	**= leisure activities**
11	**= sport**
111	**= individual sports**
112	**= team sports**
112.1	**= indoor team sports**
112.2	**= outdoor team sports**
112.21	**= cricket**
112.22	**= rugby football**
112.23	**= association football**

etc.

6 Alphabetical codes can be used in conjunction with any of the above to make the meaning of a code even more clear. Thus, the faceted code which we discussed could well have had the following values for its first character:

S = **screws**
N = **nuts**
B = **bolts**
etc.

While this makes a code more recognizable, it also opens up the possibility of more errors, such as 1 and I being confused, for example.

When deciding upon the coding system to use in a given set of circumstances, the systems analyst should consider the following points:

1 The code must be appropriate to the circumstances; if necessary, a **mixed code**, which combines the most suitable features of those coding systems outlined above, should be used.

2 The code opted for must be simple to use and understand.

3 It should lend itself to cost-effective computer processing, and it should be capable of being used in any related systems.

4 It should be flexible, so that fairly minor changes in the items being classified and coded do not render it useless.

5 It should lend itself to expansion.

19.5.3 Form design

When designing the forms which will be used in a system, at least four major aspects need to be considered; the printing of the forms, their completion by the clerical staff, the preparation of data from the forms, and the subsequent use of the forms, perhaps for reference. We shall make a number of general points under these four headings, although it should be remembered that the novice is well advised to consult the expert in this area of work before embarking upon form design in practice.

Printing considerations
1 Where possible, paper of standard sizes, colours and weight should be used so as to minimize costs.

2 Any special printing, such as the use of three or four colours, may make the forms easier to use, but it will also increase the cost of printing. Clearly, a compromise must be made.

3 Any rules concerning 'house style', which are laid down by the organization within which the forms will be used, should be adhered to.

4 The larger the volume of forms printed in a run, the lower will be the average cost of each form; the production of too many forms at once, however, will make the introduction of alterations more costly.

The completion of forms

5 All forms should be clearly identified with a form number on them; serial numbering may be required for control purposes.

6 Instructions should be printed on the form to enable accurate completion to be carried out.

7 As much data as possible should be pre-printed on the form, to speed up the form-filling process; data to be completed should be grouped together logically to assist the user.

8 The designer of a form should bear in mind the method of completion; a document which will be typed upon should differ from one which will be completed by hand on the factory floor. Some forms may be completed as a by-product of another operation, and this will have to be borne in mind when they are being designed.

9 The number of copies required should be carefully decided upon. Different colours may be used for the different copies, but this may increase the cost. The method of making copies should be determined.

10 When required, space should be left for signatures, dates and other items.

Data preparation considerations

11 Forms should be designed so that data preparation can be effected easily, cheaply and with as few errors as possible being made. A sensible layout allows the key operator to read from left to right and from top to bottom, so that eyeball movement and eye strain are minimized.

12 The use of colours which are easy on the eye should be adopted. Shading can be used, where appropriate, to highlight crucial fields.

13 Fields which are most often used should be grouped together at the front of the form so that the data preparation personnel do not have to 'skip' over the many blank characters which will often appear in little-used fields.

Subsequent use

14 The design of a form must be appropriate to any other uses to which it will be put, once completed. If it is to be filed, the position of any required holes will need to be considered; if it is to be mailed, envelope sizes will be relevant. Even such a mundane task as photocopying may affect the design of a form, as, of course, any colours used in its original design will lose their significance during that process. A form which is to be handled a large number of times may require heavier paper, to ensure its durability.

15 In all cases, the subsequent stages should be carefully considered, with special reference to clarity and error-free working.

19.6 Processing tasks

19.6.1 A real-time system

In a real-time system, single transactions or enquiries are dealt with as and when they occur. One program is thus able to carry out the following tasks:

1 checking the transaction, to ensure that it is a reasonable one, and reporting errors back to the operator for immediate correction; an unknown enquiry code, for example, would be rejected;
2 retrieving the appropriate record(s) from the master file(s), possibly using random access techniques, and bringing them into the CPU;
3 further checking that the transaction is still reasonable, bearing in mind the data retrieved from the master record(s); a customer wishing to withdraw cash from his/her bank account, for example, would not be allowed to do so if such a withdrawal would go beyond the allowed overdraft limit;
4 updating the master record if appropriate;
5 reporting back to the user.

19.6.2 The validate program

In a batch system, however, this is not usually the way things are done; a run cannot be halted so that a user can be informed that a few transactions among many thousands of transactions have been found to be unreasonable. This means that, if one large program is constructed which has the job of carrying out the two types of checking detailed in the previous section, as well as the updating and reporting tasks, some transaction records will be rejected as incorrect, others will be applied to the master file, and the reports produced will be a mixture of up-to-date and out-of-date information. Clearly, this is not entirely satisfactory.

One solution to this problem, which is often employed in practice, is to separate the initial checking of transactions from the updating of the master records. A separate program, known as a **validate program**, is written with the sole task of filtering out unreasonable transactions, and passing forward to the next stage only those records which are thought to be correct. Transactions which have been rejected because they are invalid can then be manually corrected and re-input to the validate program. Because the validation and updating routines are carried out by different programs, this checking and correction process can be carried out as many times as required. Eventually, a file of valid transaction records will be produced which can be passed forward to the next stage of processing (*see* Fig 19.7).

19.6.3   The sort program

What happens next in a batch processing system will depend very much upon the type of file organization opted for during the file design stage, although other factors, discussed below, may also be relevant.

If one master file is being used, and that file is a sequential file, then the valid file of transactions will have to be sorted into the same key-field sequence as the master file. If the reason for this is not absolutely clear to the reader, then the section on sequential processing in Chapter 6 should be carefully re-scrutinized. After sorting, the transaction file can be applied to the master file in an update program, and the required reports produced (*see* Fig 19.8).

Fig 19.7   The validation process

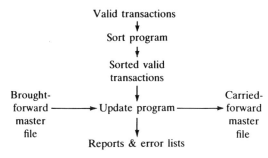

Fig 19.8   *Sorting and updating*

19.6.4   The print program

Of course, such an approach ignores the rejection of those transactions only found to be invalid at the update stage, parts which are out of stock, for instance. If this is a significant problem, then the updating and report-producing functions can be divided up between two programs. This will allow the rejections from the update program to be corrected and recycled through the whole of the validate, sort and update processes. Only when a clean master file has been produced will it be put through a separate print program (*see* Fig 19.9). The cost implications of this must be carefully thought out, however,

There are, in fact, other reasons why such an approach might be opted for, but we shall delay a consideration of these until we discuss systems flowcharting in the next section.

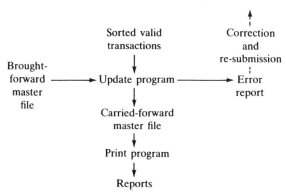

Fig 19.9   *The print program*

19.6.5   A low hit-rate batch system

The considerations concerning sorting dealt with in the preceding subsections are relevant only to a system which is built around a sequential master file. Where a batch system uses a direct access file, there is no need to sort the transactions prior to the updating of the master file. In such a case, the processing steps could take the form shown in Fig 19.10.

Such a system, however, would produce output in a haphazard sequence. While this approach will sometimes be satisfactory, there will be occasions when it will not. In such cases, it will be necessary to either sort the transactions to the required sequence *before* applying them to the master file, much as we did in the sequentially-organized system above, or to separate the updating and printing functions, taking care to sort the output *in between* the two resulting programs. Clearly, cost considerations will determine the approach which is opted for in a given set of circumstances. We shall develop this point further when we consider systems flow-charting in the next section.

19.6.6   More complex systems

Clearly, systems which involve more than one master file will be rather more complex than those outlined. Before attempting a discussion of such systems, however, we need to be able to understand the charts which computer personnel use to represent the major processing tasks carried out by a system. These are known as systems flowcharts, and they are dealt with in the following section.

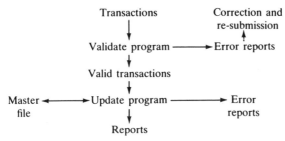

Fig 19.10   The low hit-rate batch system

19.7   Systems flowcharts

19.7.1   The nature of a systems flowchart

A systems flowchart is a diagram which gives an **overall** view of a
data processing system. It does this by showing:

● the **tasks** carried out within such a system, either by manual
  means or by the computer
● and the **devices** and **media** used to hold the files which enter and
  are output from the system, as well as those used as working
  files within the system

19.7.2   A flowchart example

We begin our consideration of systems flowcharts by looking at a
simple example. Suppose that we have been asked to draw the
systems flowchart for a weekly payroll system, which produces
payslips in employee number sequence. We can summarize the
points which we have made about systems design by asking the
following questions:

What is the **nature** of the system?
What is the **frequency** of **output**?
What **output medium** should we use?
What is the **hit-rate** on the **master file(s)**?
What type of **file organization** is, therefore, appropriate?
What **file medium** should we use?
What is the **frequency of input**?
What **input medium** should we employ?
What **processing tasks** need to be carried out, and what **programs**
do we need?

If we attempt to answer these questions in relation to the payroll
system outlined above, we come up with the following points:
Nature: because employees have to be paid once a week, the system
will be a cyclic, or periodic, one. **Batch processing** will be
appropriate.
Output frequency: the output is required once a week.
Medium/device: the line printer would appear to be an appropriate
device to use.
Master file(s) hit-rate: the hit-rate on the master file will be high,

as nearly every record, if not all of them, will need to be accessed and processed each week.

File organization: in such a case, sequential organization will be the most cost-effective. Employee number order can be used.

File medium: magnetic disk will be used, with updating by copying opted for as a security measure.

Input frequency: weekly input, tying in with weekly output, is appropriate.

Medium/device: several of the input methods discussed in Chapter 4 would be appropriate here. Let us opt for key to disk.

Processing tasks and programs:

1   Key and verify the data, using time sheets as the source documents.

2   Check the raw data in a **validate program**, reporting errors as they are found, and passing forward to a working file those records which appear to be correct.

3   Correct and re-submit records which the validate program has found to be incorrect.

4   Use a **sort program** to sort the records found to be valid into the same sequence as the sequentially-held master file, namely employee number sequence.

5   In an update program:

●   apply the sorted transactions file to the brought-forward master file, producing a carried-forward master file

●   check, as the master file is updated, that the transactions are consistent with the master records, reporting any errors found for subsequent manual investigation and correction

●   produce the payslips

19.7.3   A flowcharted solution

Let us now see how the processing tasks described above would be depicted in a systems flowchart (*see* Fig 19.11). The following points should be noted. The numbers shown on the chart would *not* usually be there; they are used here to allow the points which follow to be more easily made.

1   The timesheets (1) enter the system as handwritten or typed entries on pieces of paper. These are the source documents. The symbol shown should be used whenever a document is in use.

2   The symbol for on-line keying is shown in box 2.

Payroll
GCL 010499

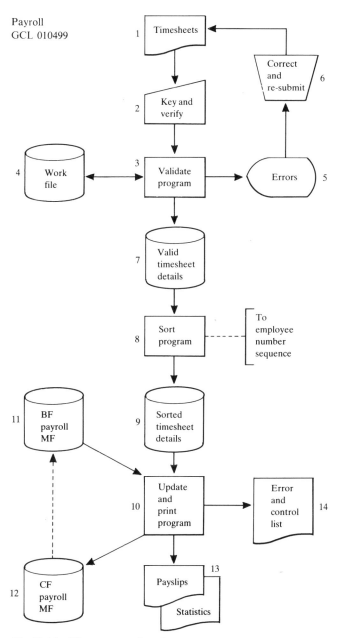

Fig 19.11   The systems flowchart

3   The keyed input enters directly into the validate program. As we have seen, this program attempts to check that there are no errors in the raw data entering the system; how it does so, and what the contents of the 'error and control list' are, will be dealt with in Section 19.8 of this chapter. The rectangle should be used to depict a program on a systems flowchart.

4   The data which is found to be reasonable is written to a work file on a disk (4).

5   Any errors detected by the validate routine are displayed on a screen (5). Some errors will be capable of being corrected immediately, others will require reference back to the user department for their correction.

6   In either case, errors are corrected and re-submitted. The manual operation symbol (6) is shown.

7   Valid items still need to be verified, as hours entered as 43 on the source document could have been keyed into the system as 34: one is right and one is wrong – but both are valid.

8   When all the input details have been keyed, validated and verified, they are retrieved from the work file, and sorted by program (8) into the same sequence as the master file, and a sorted valid transactions file is written to magnetic disk (9).

9   The transactions file is then applied to the brought-forward master file (11), which was produced during the last processing cycle, and a carried-forward version of the master file is produced (12). The update program (10) produces the payslips (13) in the required sequence. A list of errors found during updating (14) is also produced; for both reports, the document symbol is again used.

In each case, note how the name of the file is written inside the appropriate symbol for the device and medium which is in use. Note also how a brief description of each process is written inside the appropriate box.

19.7.4   The print program

We saw, when we were discussing systems design in Section 19.6, that it is possible to carry out the updating and printing process in two distinct programs, so that errors found by the update can be corrected and re-submitted. A further reason for the use of this approach concerns the following two factors:

1   Updating is a complex task involving reading, calculating, checking and writing. This means that an update program is a large program.

2 Printing of, for example, thousands of payslips will be (by the standards of the computer) a very slow process. If 10 000 payslips, each with ten lines of print, are produced on a line printer which works at 2000 LPM, then it will take 50 minutes (10 000 × 10 ÷ 2000) for the information to be output.

Taken together, these considerations mean that a program which combines *both* the update and the print functions will be large and slow. This will hinder an installation's attempts to use a multi-

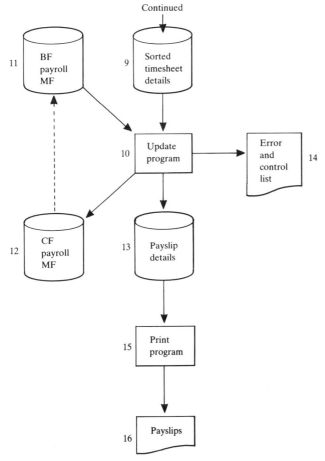

Fig 19.12   Using a print program

programming environment efficiently, as much memory will be occupied for a long time.

A better approach could well be to use an update program which writes its output to a magnetic medium, and a separate print program which reads this file in order to produce payslips. The update will still be a large program, but it will work much faster using a magnetic medium for output. The print program, on the other hand, will still work slowly but, as it only reads and prints, it will be very small. Computer managers do not like large, slow programs, but they are not too concerned about small, slow programs, or large, fast ones!

Using this approach, boxes 9 onwards on our chart could take the form shown in Fig 19.12.

A further point to note is that both of the charts which we have drawn so far will produce output in the same sequence as the master file, namely employee number sequence. This approach will often be satisfactory but, if there are tens of thousands of employees, all scattered across a large site or across several sites, then the distribution of the payslips could well be very difficult indeed.

One answer is to sort the output into employee within department sequence before printing it. Consider Fig 19.13 which uses this approach.

19.7.5   A second example

Now that we are familiar with the basics of systems flowcharting, we are in a position to tackle a second example.

Problem
Draw a systems flowchart for a system which carries out the following tasks:

1   A file of transactions is read each week; there is a record for each item of stock which has left a store during the week; there are usually several thousand records in the file.
2   The transactions are validated and then applied to a master file which contains many hundreds of thousands of stock records.
3   A report is printed which contains a line for each item of stock which has been active during the week. The reports are required in part number order.

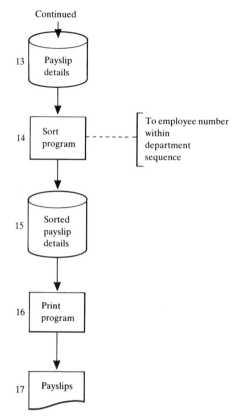

Fig 19.13   Sorting print details

As a first step towards drawing the above chart, attempt to complete the checklist which we developed above in 19.7.2, before carrying on reading.

Your checklist should take the following form:

Nature: because weekly reporting is required, rather than reports which are produced as events happen, the system is a batch system.

Output frequency: weekly.

Medium: line printer stationery.

Master file(s) hit-rate: low.

File organization: random.

Medium: magnetic disk will be needed.

Input frequency: weekly.

Medium: key-to-disk.

Tasks and programs: the records will be keyed, validated and

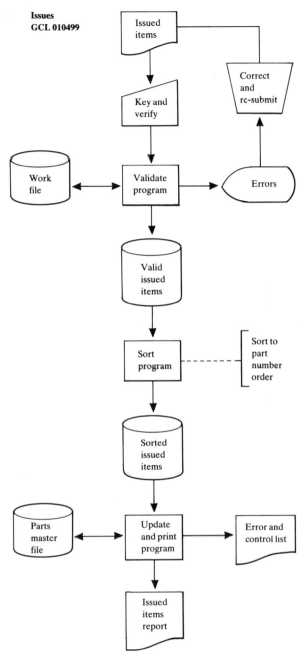

Fig 19.14   A low hit-rate system

verified using the key-to-disk system. Manual corrections will be made as required. Completed batches of work will then be written to a transfer file on disk. The transfer file could then be sorted, so that the output will be in the required sequence, and applied to the master file. When the disk file is updated, updating in place is used. The update program produces the (low volume) output.

Make sure that you understand each of the points made above before you attempt to draw the chart. When you have completed the chart scrutinize the suggested solution in Fig 19.14.

Note that we do not need to sort the transactions file for the purpose of accessing the master file, because the parts file is randomly organized.

The sorting shown in the flowchart in Fig 19.14 is done so that the output is easier for the recipients to handle and use.

Note also that only one disk symbol is used in respect of the parts master file. This is because **updating in place** is being used.

19.7.6   A third example

Let us look at a third example.

Problem
Draw a systems flowchart for a system which produces invoices each week. Assume that most customers are active each week, but that relatively few parts are sold in each period.

Once again, you should attempt to complete the checklist before carrying on reading, first considering how many master files the system will need to use!

Clearly, this system will need to access and update both a **customer master file** and a **stock master file** so that invoices can be produced. This being the case, the checklist will take the form:
Nature: a batch system.
Output frequency: weekly.
Medium: stationery.
Master file(s) hit-rate: customer file – high, stock file – low.
File organization: customer file – sequential, stock file – random.
Medium: customer file – magnetic disk, stock file – magnetic disk.
Input frequency: weekly.
Medium: key-to-disk.
Tasks and programs: the records will be keyed, validated and verified using the key-to-disk system, as in the previous example.

Invoicing system
GCL 010499

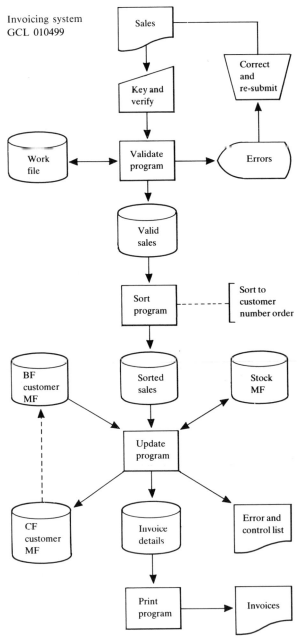

Fig 19.15 A system with two master files

Because the customer master file is a sequential file, the transactions will next need to be sorted into customer number sequence. In the update program, the customer file can then be read in the normal way and, as this is happening, the appropriate records can be brought from the stock file using a randomizing algorithm. This will allow:

- invoices to be output, line by line, for subsequent printing
- the stock records to be updated
- the customer records to be updated

Once the above points have been grasped, an attempt should be made to draw the required systems flowchart. Do not look at the chart in Fig 19.15 until you have made such an attempt.

19.7.7   A fourth example

A fourth example follows.

Problem
Draw a systems flowchart for a system which produces invoices each week. Assume that relatively few customers and relatively few parts are active each week.

Attempt to complete the checklist before consulting the one which follows.

Nature: a batch system.
Output frequency: weekly.
Medium: stationery.
Master file(s) hit-rate: customer file − low, stock file − low.
File organization: both files − random.
Medium: both files − disk.
Input frequency: weekly.
Medium: key-to-tape.
Tasks and programs: the raw data will need to be validated, as in the previous examples. Because the master files are both randomly organized, it will not be necessary to sort the transactions in order cost-effectively to access records. But if a sort is not used, a customer who has bought several items during the period could then receive several invoices instead of one, as the transactions will be fed to the update program haphazardly. Consider the following

Invoicing
GCL 010499

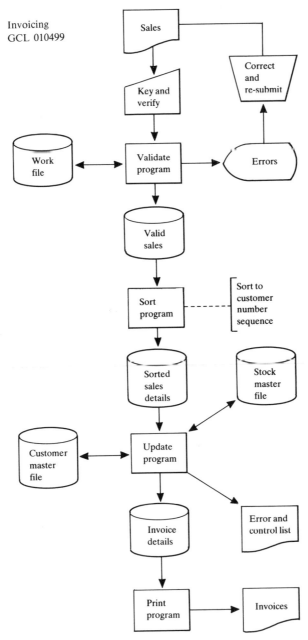

Fig 19.16   Two low hit-rate files

example:

transaction for customer 12437   part 19682
transaction for customer 69182   part 67021
transaction for customer 12437   part 96187 ... etc.

Clearly, the invoice for customer 69182 will have to be printed
between the two invoices for customer 12437. To avoid this, the
transactions could be sorted to customer order between the validate
and update programs; all the items relating to customer 12437 will
then be in sequence when the transactions file is read into the
update program, and so one invoice can be produced.

Another possible solution would be to separate the updating and
printing tasks, and have a program for each function.

The update could then output 'print images' to a magnetic disk
file. Records thus output would contain the data needed for an
invoice to be printed. If the records were sorted before going into
the print program, one invoice per customer could be produced.
The problem with this latter approach, however, is that multiple
transactions by the same customer lead to multiple master file
accesses.

Attempt to draw a systems flowchart which uses the former
approach before examining a suggested solution to the problem
(*see* Fig 19.16).

19.7.8   A fifth example

A fifth problem runs as follows.

Problem
Draw a systems flowchart for a system which produces invoices
each month. Most customers and most parts are active each
month.

Attempt to complete the checklist before examining the one
depicting a possible solution to the problem.

Nature: a batch system.
Output frequency: monthly.
Medium: stationery.
Master file(s) hit-rate: customer file – high, stock file – high.
File organization: both files – sequential.

Medium: both files — magnetic disk.
Input frequency: monthly.
Medium: key-to-disk.
Tasks and programs: the records will be keyed, validated and verified using the key-to-disk system, as in the previous examples. Because both master files are sequentially organized, it will be necessary to sort the transactions, in order to carry out the updating function. But, of course, we cannot sort the transaction into *both* customer number sequence *and* part number *at once*. Nor can we update *both* master files *at once* when they are both held sequentially, as a customer whose record is near to the start of the customer master file may well have purchased a part whose record is near the end of the part file! For this reason *two* sorts and *two* updates are required. If we update the customer file second, then that update program can also produce the invoices; this ensures that each customer only receives one invoice. If we left the updating of the stock file to the last, then a customer would receive one invoice for each part purchased in the period.

You should attempt to draw a systems flowchart from the above checklist before examining the suggested solution shown in Fig 19.17.

Because this is the first chart which we have looked at which shows the updating of the stock and customer master files in *separate* programs, we have now encountered a problem which we did not come across when *both* files were accessed in *one* program.

How can we produce an invoice line in the *second* update program, when such items as the price and the description of the stock item are held on the master file which is accessed by the *first* update program?

The answer, as the reader will perhaps have deduced, is that the output from the first update program is the original transaction *plus* those details, such as unit price and description, which will be needed for the production of the invoice line. Thus, to simplify, the fields on the transactions input to the first update program could be:

Customer number
Part number
Quantity

and the fields on the records which are output by the first update

Invoicing
GCL 010499

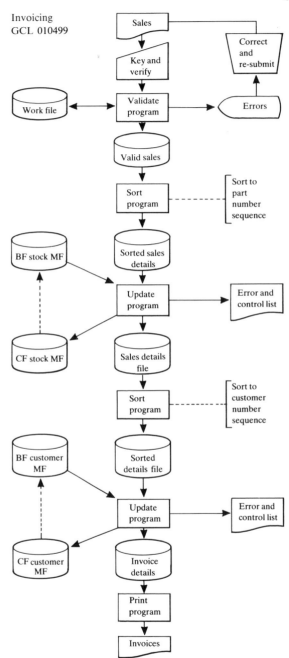

Fig 19.17   Two high hit-rate files

could be:

Customer number
Part number
Quantity
Description
Unit price

The two extra fields have been copied from the stock master file, so that the second update program can use them in updating the customer master file and in producing the invoices.

19.7.9   Problems involving two charts

An examination question could pose a problem which would need the drawing of two separate systems flowcharts.

Consider the following example. A company stocks 50 000 parts. A list is required each month of active parts. In any given month, most parts are active. Prior to the monthly parts list run, a file maintenance run takes place. This allows changes to be made to existing stock records, new records to be inserted onto the file, and records relating to discontinued lines to be deleted from the file. In a typical month, there are 500 such changes.

Flowchart the monthly processing. Attempt to flowchart the monthly file maintenance and file updating before reading further.

It is hoped that the reader will have reasoned along the following lines:

1   Two flowcharts are needed, one for the file maintenance run, and one for the update run.
2   Because the hit-rate is low during the file maintenance run, and high during the file updating, then indexed-sequential file organization will be appropriate.

If your answer does not take account of these factors, then you should re-attempt it before looking at Fig 19.18 and Fig 19.19.

19.7.10   Real-time system flowcharts

It will be apparent to the reader that the batch approach shown in the flowcharts which we have examined so far has severe limitations. One of these concerns the difficulties of achieving a satisfactory interface between the clerical aspects of a system and its

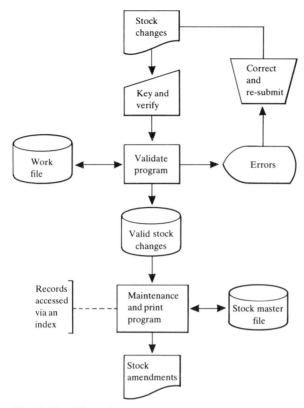

Fig 19.18   File maintenance

computerized aspects. If the clerical staff have taken an order, then they could well find, perhaps days later when the batch processing system is run, that the product in question is out-of-stock, or that the customer who has placed the order is over his credit limit. What is to be done?

An answer, of course, is the use of a real-time system. This will allow the clerk to establish, *as he/she takes the order*, that all is well. The construction of real-time system flowcharts is the subject matter of the next subsection.

19.7.11   A real-time example

Problem
Draw a systems flowchart for a stock recording system. The system allows remote transactions to be applied to the master file as and

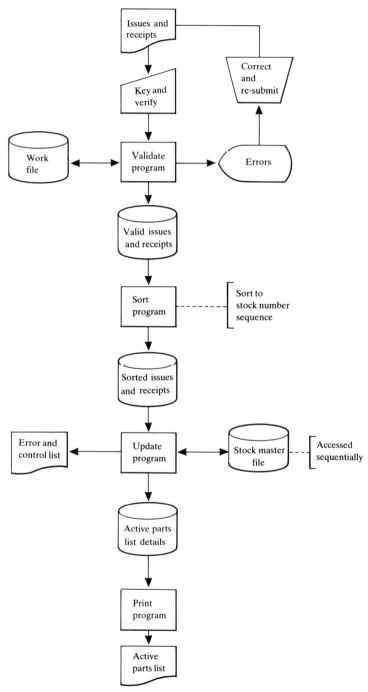

Fig 19.19   File updating

when they happen, and enquiries to be made of the stock file at any time, with immediate response.

Attempt to complete the flowchart checklist before looking at the completed checklist below.

Nature: a real-time system, which requires an immediate updating of master records, and an immediate response to enquiries.

Output frequency: on demand.

Medium/device: a visual display unit would be appropriate.

Master file hit-rate: very low, as transactions will be processed on a one-off basis.

File organization: random organization.

Medium: magnetic disk.

Input frequency: on demand.

Medium/device: dual purpose input/output devices would be appropriate, as above.

Tasks and programs: operators would key in transactions and enquiries directly to the system via a keyboard. As each entry is dealt with individually by the system, rather than as an item in a large batch, one program carrying out the checking, updating and reporting functions would seem appropriate; *see* 19.6.1. Clearly, no sort is required.

The systems flowchart for the system developed above is shown in Fig 19.20.

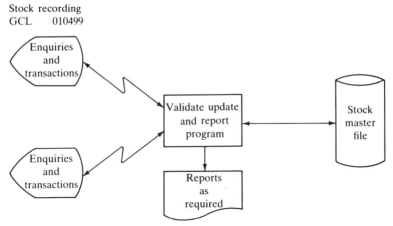

Stock recording
GCL   010499

Fig 19.20   A real-time system

19.7.12   A second real-time example

Attempt to flowchart the following system before looking at Fig 19.21.

1   As orders are taken over the telephone, they are keyed directly into a computer. Any errors detected by the program are reported at once so that they can be dealt with straight away.

2   If an order appears valid, then the stock master file is accessed in order to ensure that the item is not out of stock. If there are any problems, then the operator is alerted at once, so that the customer can be informed and, where appropriate, offered an alternative.

3   If there are still no problems, then the customer master file is accessed so that the customer's position concerning credit limit can be ascertained. Again, any problems are immediately reported so that they can be actioned.

4   Where no difficulties are encountered, the customer file and the stock file are updated, and a despatch note is printed on a printer in the stores. An invoice is also printed.

5   Details of cash received from customers, details concerning

Order system
GCL   010499

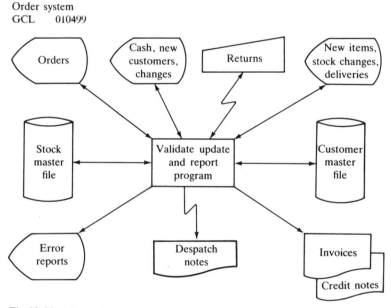

Fig 19.21   An order system

new customers, and any changes concerning the fields on a customer's record are keyed in, and are used to update the customer master file.

6   When customers return goods, the details are keyed in from the stores so that the system can update both files. Credit notes are printed.

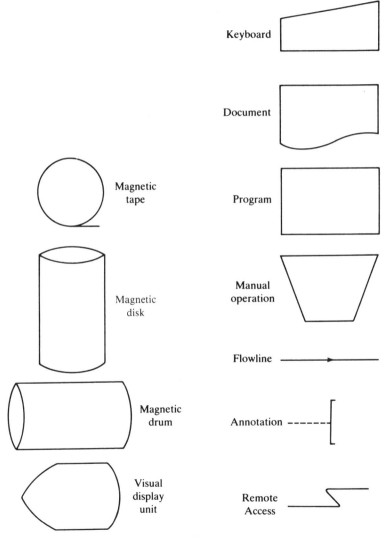

Fig 19.22   Systems flowchart symbols

7 Data concerning new items which have been added to stock, changes to existing stock items, and deliveries of items are keyed into the system, so that the stock file can be updated.

19.7.13 Systems flowcharts – a summary

We have seen that a systems flowchart gives an *overall* view of a data processing system. It does this by showing the tasks carried out within the system and the devices and media used by the system.

Note the distinction between such a systems flowchart, and the program flowcharts dealt with in Unit 3; each program depicted in a systems flowchart, apart from items of standard software such as sorts, needs to be charted in program flowchart form to show *how* it will carry out the tasks allotted to it.

When drawing systems flowcharts, the symbols shown in Fig 19.22 are used.

Systems flowcharts, like all charts, should be titled and dated.

19.8 Control aspects of systems design

19.8.1 The need for accuracy control

When a data processing task is undertaken manually, the human beings carrying out the job will naturally use their common sense; for example, they would automatically reject input which states that an employee has worked 150 hours in a week and they would query output which quoted a payment of minus £10 on an invoice.

When a task is computerized, however, the picture changes somewhat. The computer, as we know, will do exactly what we tell it, but it will do only what we tell it. In other words, raw data is input to a system, it is processed according to the rules laid down in the programs which handle it, and information is the result. Unless we specifically ask the computer to report on items such as the absurd ones detailed above, the machine will happily accept them!

In this section, we examine ways in which the systems analyst can build accuracy checks into systems, so that he does not suffer from 'garbage in, garbage out'. We look first at the controls used in a typical batch processing system, and then at those which can be employed in a real-time environment.

19.8.2 Checks in the validate program

The checks which can be specified by a systems analyst for inclusion in a batch processing system's validate, or data vet, program can be divided into four types:

● character checks
● field checks
● record checks
● checks applied to a batch or a file of records as a whole

Such checks are discussed further below.

Character checks

Format (or picture) tests
Certain characters, for example digits in a price, must always be numeric. Other characters, perhaps part of a product name, must always be alphabetic. Yet other characters, such as those in a surname, cannot be numeric. Where such criteria can be determined, the validate program can be written to report upon illegal characters.

Special characters
A character may have to be one of a particular set. A given character in a record, for example, may have to be either blank or contain a minus sign; a character denoting marital status may have to be equal to S, M, W or D. Again, illegal characters can be reported.

Presence tests
A character may have to be present in order that a record is meaningful.

Field checks

Size tests
Often, a field must be a certain number of characters in length. An account number, for example, is perhaps always eight digits long. Any deviation above or below this will be reported.

Limit tests
These tests are designed to enable fields above (or below) certain

pre-determined values to be highlighted. Examples are the reporting of overtime hours entered as more than, say, 50 per week, or salary less than a certain value.

Range tests
Where a field can be checked against both lower and upper limits, a range test is being used. An obvious example is an employee's age which must be 16 or over, but not more than 65.

Special values
In certain circumstances, a field may have to hold a value which is one of a particular set. If a five-letter department code is used, for example, it might have to be MRKTG, PRDTN, CMPTR or another pre-determined code. The month in a date must be between 1 and 12 inclusive, and it must be an integer.

Presence tests
Certain fields must be present to make a record meaningful. An account number is an example.

Self-checking numbers
It is important that every field on a record input to a data processing system is correct, and the tests detailed in this section try to ensure this. It could be argued, however, that the most important field on any input record is its key field. If, for example, a customer number is wrong on input to the updating procedure, then not only will the customer who made the transaction not have it recorded on the master record, but we may incorrectly update the master record of a customer who had nothing to do with the purchase, and this customer will not take kindly to that!

For this reason, check digits are used on important fields such as key fields.

The types of errors made when transcribing numeric fields to machine-sensible form can be of the following kinds:

Error	Example
Transcription	12345 becomes 12545
Transposition	12345 becomes 12435
Double transposition	12345 becomes 12543
Omission	12345 becomes 1345
Addition	12345 becomes 123745
Random	A combination of two or more of the above, or any other error

A check digit is a self-checking digit which tries to overcome some of the above errors. When a new customer or employee is taken on, (s)he is allocated a reference number; let us say that this is 1234. A human operator then calculates the check-digit, using a formula, **from the other digits in the key field**; let us assume that this works out at 3. The reference number, or key field, then becomes the five-digit number 12343. On input, the validate program, using the same formula, checks that the check digit 3 is correct with regard to the other four digits in the number. An error will be reported and will cause the record to be rejected.

The efficiency of a system of check digits will depend on the formula used to create them. Let us examine some of the issues involved.

The simplest way to calculate a check digit is to add up the individual digits in the number, disregard the 'tens' position, and use the 'units' in the answer as the check digit. Thus 12345 adds up to 15, and so it would become 123455. But this does not spot transposition errors, as 12345 has the same check digit as 13245.

If we weight the digits, each with a different weight, and multiply them by their weights before doing the addition, we overcome this. Let us give the rightmost digit a weight of 2, the next 3, and so on, so that 1234 is dealt with thus:

$$1 \times 5 = \quad 5$$
$$2 \times 4 = \quad 8$$
$$3 \times 3 = \quad 9$$
$$4 \times 2 = \quad \underline{8}$$
$$\qquad\qquad 30$$

1234 becomes 12340

We are, in effect, dividing by 10 and using the remainder as the check digit.

Weighted check digit calculation will thus spot transposition errors, but some transcription errors will slip through. If the data preparation operator, for example, keyed 12340 as 72340, the calculation in the data vet program would be

$$(7 \times 5 + 2 \times 4 + 3 \times 3 + 4 \times 2) = 60$$

After division, a check digit of 0 appears correct, and so the error is not reported. The reason for this error going unnoticed is that the difference between the erroneous digit and the correct digit, when multiplied by its weight, is a multiple of the divisor. In other words:

$(7 - 1) \times 5$ is a multiple of 10

We can overcome this by using 11 as the divisor, as no two single digits multiplied together ever give a multiple of 11. This 'Modulus 11' system is very common:

(a)   multiply the least significant (rightmost) digit in the number by 2, the next by 3, and so on
(b)   add up the results
(c)   divide by 11
(d)   if the remainder is 0, this is the check digit
(e)   otherwise subtract the remainder from 11 and use this as the check digit, 10 counting as X:

$$1234 \text{ gives} \quad 1 \times 5 = \quad 5$$
$$2 \times 4 = \quad 8$$
$$3 \times 3 = \quad 9$$
$$4 \times 2 = \quad \underline{8}$$
$$30 \div 11 = 2, \text{ remainder } 8$$

giving a digit check of 3

On input of the number, the validate program merely multiplies all five digits by their weights, the weight for the check digit being 1, and the result of the addition should be exactly divisible by 11.

This method detects all the errors listed above except random errors, some of which will slip through.

Record checks

Field inter-relationship tests
Each field in a transaction may be perfectly correct in its own right, but it may be the case that when a field is checked in relation to another field, or other fields, it is apparent that something is amiss. A title set to MISS on a new employee's input record, for example, is perfectly reasonable; so is a sex code set to M. Taken together, however, it would appear that something is not quite right! The validate program could carry out such a consistency check and report any such cases. The only limit upon the inclusion of such tests is the ingenuity of the systems designer.

Batch or file checks

Sequence tests
In certain accounting systems, it may be possible to check that transactions in a file are in consecutive sequence of serial number.

Transaction counts
As transaction records are created by the clerical staff responsible for their origination, a **count** is made of the number of transactions in the file. A dummy record is then created and placed at the end of the genuine records; this control record, or trailer record, will contain, inter alia, the count of transactions made for control purposes. When the transactions are prepared for input to the computer, perhaps by being keyed onto disk, the control record is also keyed. As the validate program reads the transactions in order to check them, it also counts them. At the end of the file, when the trailer record is recognized, the program checks that the number of transactions which it has read is equal to the number which the clerical staff entered into the control record. Any discrepancy will need to be followed up, as it may indicate the loss of one or more transactions, or the inclusion of extra transactions, during the data preparation.

The use of one control record at the end of a file of transactions will be satisfactory only when a small number of transactions is being dealt with. Where many transactions enter a batch processing system each time it is run, it is usual to divide those transactions up into **batches**. Each batch will have its own batch control record, and the validate program will check the record count in each of these control records. When an error is found, it is thus much easier for the clerical staff to take corrective action.

Batch totals
To illustrate the importance of the use of batch totals, let us consider a simple example.

Assume that a clerk has originated three source documents, each containing a field which holds the number of hours which an employee has worked in a week.

Suppose further that, when the source documents are keyed on to disk, both the operator who keys the data and the person carrying out the verification process mistake the value in the middle document and a transcription error thus takes place. Suppose also that the error leaves the field valid.

If nothing further were done to control the data going into the system, the error would slip through, as the hours would appear correct to the validate program, being an entirely reasonable number of hours for a person to work in a week.

Fortunately, however, we can take measures to prevent such an event happening. As the clerks enter the hours into the source documents, they total them. When the dummy records which we encountered above are created at the end of each batch, these totals are entered into them. The dummy records are then keyed, along with the genuine data records.

As the validate program reads the transactions, it also totals up the hours fields. At the end of each batch, when the trailer record is recognized, the program checks that the total which it has accumulated equals the total which the clerical staff entered into the batch control record. Discrepancies are reported for following up.

Any field which is considered sufficiently important can be controlled in a trailer record in this way.

Hash totals

Often, batch totals are made for control purposes of items such as hours worked, balances outstanding, or quantities in stock; such totals are meaningful in their own right. Sometimes, however, it is required to control fields such as dates of birth, account numbers or even pack sizes. Where batch totals are made of items which it would normally be meaningless to sum, use is being made of a **hash total** for control purposes. Even alphabetic fields can be added to give a hash total for checking if a conversion process is first carried out.

Batch number checks

Each record in a batch may have the number of the batch entered into it, so that the validate program can check that each transaction belongs to the batch in question.

Any errors found by the validate program are reported on the 'error and control list' for subsequent investigation and correction by the clerical staff.

19.8.3   Checks in the update program

As we have seen, it is the task of the validate program to check for errors in the raw data entering a computer system. Certain errors, however, will not be detectable at that early stage; only when a file of transactions is applied to a master file will it be evident, for example, that a sale has been made to a non-existent customer. We now consider the tests that can be written into an update program.

Matching checks

When a transaction is encountered which purports to be an insertion, perhaps relating to a new employee, the update program checks that a record for an employee with the same reference number is not already on the file. When an amendment is read, a master record must exist to be amended. Similarly, when a deletion is input, perhaps signifying that an existing product has been discontinued, a record for that product must be on the master file.

Consistency checks

Checks can be carried out by the update program to ensure that transactions are consistent with what is already held on the master records. Customers, for example, can be checked to be within their credit limits, quantities held cannot become negative, and employees aged 25 may not retire on pension.

Checks digits

Transaction records passed forward from the validate program will have fields with checks digits in them. These can be re-checked by the update program to ensure that no corruption has occurred between the validate and update stages.

Master file records, too, will have their key fields protected by check digits; these will be checked.

Trailer records

The file of valid records passed forward from the validate program will almost certainly have a trailer record at its end which contains a record count and totals of important fields. These will be checked by the update program to ensure that nothing has been lost, perhaps during the sorting phase.

Similarly, the master file which the update reads will also have a control record at its end which was created during the last processing cycle. This will be checked.

The update program will also need to write a trailer record forward, containing totals and a count, for checking next time.

Any errors found by the update program are reported on an error and control list for investigation and correction by the clerical staff.

19.8.4   Checks in a real-time system

Special problems arise when the control aspects of a real-time system are considered. Often, the operators entering enquiries and transactions are geographically scattered, and so supervision is less easy. Verification is not usually undertaken and, as the entries are made individually on a one-off basis, batch controls cannot be used.

On the other hand, if errors in the input can be found, then they can be reported to the operator in real-time for immediate correction.

We examine below some of the checks that can be incorporated into a real-time system:

● Character checks
● Field checks
● Record checks

The checks detailed in section 19.8.2 under the above three headings can be used in a real-time system.

● Matching checks
● Consistency checks
● Check digits

The checks detailed in section 19.8.3 under the above three headings can be used in a real-time system.

In addition the following checks can be used:

Descriptive read-back
When an operator requesting an item keys in its reference number, a mistake may be made. The error may possibly go unnoticed, despite the checks specified above. One way to reduce the likelihood of such an event happening is for the program dealing with the transaction to give an alphabetic read-back of the item's name, perhaps on a VDU screen. Thus an operator meaning to key in product code 123456, because he requires a dozen footballs, would expect to see the word 'Footballs' displayed on the screen. If the product code is accidentally keyed in as 123567, then (s)he will be made aware of the error when a message such as, for example, 'Lacrosse sticks' appears instead. The operator will then be able to correct the mistake.

Group checks
Under certain circumstances, it will be possible to check a group of transactions. In a bank, for example, an interim cash balance can be output at intervals, for checking against the cash held.

Identity checks
The system can be designed to check the identity of a particular user, perhaps using a password, a special badge, or even by recognizing the user's voice; a particular terminal can be identified for control purposes, too. Input from unacceptable operators or terminals can thus be rejected.

Others
Many other types of checks can be used. Some systems keep a record of operator errors for subsequent reporting to management; this is thought to be an incentive for the operators!

19.9   The systems specification

19.9.1   The place of the specification

At the end of the systems design stage, the analyst documents the proposals in a **systems specification**. This is also called:

- a systems definition
- a systems report
- a systems proposal

19.9.2   The functions of the specification

The systems definition attempts to carry out the following functions.

The 'contract'
As the specification acts as the final definitive statement of the clerical and computerized procedures making up the new system, it acts as a 'contract' between the staff of the EDP department and the user department. The costs and benefits expected from the development, implementation and running of the proposed system must thus be quantified to enable a sound decision to be made at this stage.

Of course, the user must make sure that the system cost-effectively does what is required before deciding to be bound to a contract.

A reference document
The definition acts as a reference document during the development, testing and implementation stages. When any dispute arises between the computer staff and the user department staff, it is the systems specification which has to be taken as an authoritative statement of what has been agreed

The procedures manual
Before a new system goes live, a procedures manual, laying down how the clerical staff should make the new system work, has to be produced. A well-written systems specification can act as the basis of such a manual.

The operating manual
In a similar fashion, the systems report can act as the basis of the operating manual which guides the operators when they are running the programs which make up the system.

19.9.3   The contents of the specification

Every computer department has its own ideas as to what details should go into a systems specification, and no two reports will be exactly alike. The following information, however, will usually be included:

1 *Introduction*   The introduction should include all the necessary background details required to enable the system to be placed into context. The system's objectives, and an overall description of how those objectives are achieved, should be documented. The place of the system in the organization's total system should be described.
2 *Justification*   The costs and the benefits of the new system should be quantified and detailed. As more work has been done on the system, these estimates will be better ones than those made during the project feasibility stage.
3 *Systems description*   The clerical and computer procedures involved in the system should be described. Narrative and flow-charts should be used as appropriate.

4 *Input*   The input will be described. Where appropriate, the source documents, from which raw data in a machine-sensible form will be prepared for input to the system, will be described; samples of the forms which the clerical staff will be asked to complete, or to work from, will be included. Volumes expected will be specified.

5 *Files*   The media on which files will be held, and the file organization which will be used, will be specified. The records to be found within the files, and the fields to be found within those records, will be laid down.

6 *Output*   A description will need to be given of every report produced by the system. A sample of each report, perhaps printed on computer stationery by a general-purpose print program, should be included. Volumes expected, and the action to be taken in both normal and exceptional circumstances, should be detailed.

7 *Controls*   The controls which will be built into the system, and the action that error reports will lead to, should be documented.

8 *Implementation*   Details of how the new system is to be implemented, including the costs involved and the implications for the clerical staff, should be included.

9 *Equipment*   The hardware and the ancillary equipment needed for the take-on and the running of the new system should be listed.

10 *Glossary*   A glossary of all the special terms used in the report should appear at its close.

19.9.4   Acceptance of the specification

The specification acts as the final definitive statement of what the new computer system will do; it must therefore be accepted by the following staff:

- the management of the department(s) which will be responsible for running the system
- the management of any other departments who will be affected, either during the setting-up stage or during live running
- the management of the computing function
- the steering committee
- the auditors
- the chief accountant

Once the systems proposal has been accepted by all of those involved, the development and implementation of the new system can begin. This is dealt with in the next chapter.

19.10   Summary

Once an area of an organization's work has been thoroughly investigated, the systems analyst is in a position to design a new, computerized, system which will carry out that work. The proposals for
the new system are documented in a systems specification; this
report has to be approved by various interested parties before the
development and implementation of the new system can go ahead.

Questions

Note that the answers to selected questions are given in the
Appendix at the end of the volume.

True or false?
I   Payroll systems are usually batch processing systems.
2   A system which produces invoices each week is an example of a
real-time system.
3   Airline reservation systems are usually batch systems.
4   A file's hit-rate refers to the number of records which are
accessed in one run.
5   So that records can be accessed quickly in a real-time situation,
magnetic tape backing storage is usually used.
6   When random organization is used, magnetic tape is
inappropriate.
7   A high hit-rate batch system will normally use a sequentially-
organized file.
8   Batch systems never use magnetic disk as a backing storage
medium.
9   Sequential files may be held on disk.
10   Batch systems never involve the use of low hit-rate master files.
11   When using disks for random processing, updating by copying is
usually used.
12   Magnetic tape updating usually involves copying data onto a
carried-forward master file.
13   A field which must always contain alphabetic characters can be
checked using a format test.
14   When a source document field containing 76543 is keyed as
75643, then a transcription error has been made.
15   When, for control purposes, the 'total age' of all the people
whose details are being input to a system is calculated, then a hash
total is being used.

16 A validate program will spot all the errors in a batch of raw data.

17 A proposed new system which has been designed by a systems analyst is documented in a systems specification.

18 The prospective user of a newly-designed computer system must make sure that the system detailed in the system proposal exactly meets his/her requirements, as subsequent alterations will prove costly.

19 A clerical procedures manual has to be produced by the systems analyst before a new system becomes operational.

20 An operating manual is prepared so that the computer operations staff can run a system on the computer.

Multiple choice (*circle one letter in each*)

21 The percentage of master records accessed in a run is referred to as the file's:
- (a) transfer rate
- (b) density
- (c) hit-rate
- (d) blocking factor
- (e) file organization

22 Magnetic tape cannot cost-effectively be used to hold:
- (a) a sequential file
- (b) a random file
- (c) an indexed-sequential file
- (d) (a) + (b)
- (e) (b) + (c)

23 To give an overall view of a computerized system, which shows the tasks carried out by the system, and the devices and media used, the analyst draws:
- (a) a logic flowchart
- (b) a program flowchart
- (c) a clerical procedures flowchart
- (d) a systems flowchart
- (e) a decision table

24 In an attempt to ensure that an employee's age has been correctly keyed into a record, which of the following tests could be used:
- (a) a size test
- (b) a presence test
- (c) a consistency test
- (d) a range test
- (e) a parity check

25 Using the usual weighted Modulus 11 check digit method, what check digit would be added to the number 2468:

(a) 0
(b) 3
(c) 6
(d) 9
(e) X

Examination questions

1 What criteria relating to effective systems design should guide a systems analyst when formulating proposals for a computer-based system?

(Assume that the systems analyst works in a company where a computer has already been acquired.)

(Chartered Association of Certified Accountants)

2 Distinguish between on-line and real-time processing. Give an example of a commercial data processing application where real-time processing would be applicable and explain what characteristics make it necessary to consider this type of processing.

(Institute of Cost and Management Accountants)

3 The company for which you work uses its computer to process data for a number of accounting systems which include standard costing and budgetary control.

The chairman of the company has been informed by the data processing manager that it would be possible to produce a comprehensive 'personnel statistics' report for each accounting period.

Company information:

No. employed – approximately 20 000
No. of manufacturing cost centres – 6
No. of service department cost centres – 4.

The 20 000 includes weekly and monthly paid clerical, supervisory and managerial staff.

As senior accounting technician you are asked to assist the systems analyst in designing the layout for the report.

Using suitable headings (i.e. the analyses by which the figures are to be given) illustrate the layout of the proposed report, and comment on the conclusions which could be obtained.

4 Describe and comment on the work carried out by the systems analyst when designing the output sub-system of a large computer-based data processing application.

(Chartered Association of Certified Accountants)

5 An important factor in the operation of all data processing systems (manual, mechanized or computerized) is the type of coding employed within the organization.

What factors determine the design of effective coding systems? Illustrate your answer with examples from your own experience.

(Institute of Cost and Management Accountants)

6 (a) Identify and briefly comment on *eight* of the desirable, if not essential, features of a coding scheme.

(b) A product coding scheme is needed to meet the following specification:

- Sales analysis by product group. There are eight product groups;
- Within each product group there are currently up to 300 products;
- Some products are manufactured entirely within the company, others are always bought in their finished state from outside suppliers; some products may be both manufactured and purchased. The product code should enable these three categories to be identified;
- The code should incorporate a check digit based upon the Modulus 11 system.

Required:

- Make a clear presentation of your proposed coding scheme, stating any assumptions you have made.
- List and explain two typical codes in your scheme, proving the check digit test.

(Chartered Association of Certified Accountants)

7 (a) Prepare a checklist for the guidance of systems analysts when designing forms for use in computer systems.

(b) Using a full sheet in your answer book, make a neat sketch of your design for a computer-prepared statement of account, showing clearly *eight* data items that would be printed by the computer. Sample entries are not required.

(Chartered Association of Certified Accountants)

8 XYZ Ltd maintains its sales ledger system on a minicomputer. The sales ledger master file is held on magnetic disk. Accounts, which contain the usual standard data, are kept on a brought-forward balance basis with the total balance analysed over current month, month 1, month 2, month 3, and month 4 and over. Visual display units are employed for the entry of transaction data and for the retrieval of data for answering enquiries. A variety of printed reports is produced on the line printer.

Required:

(a)   Identify and briefly explain *five* items of transaction data which would be input to the system.

(b)   Draft, with *two* lines of sample entries, the credit limit excess and aged balance report which is produced monthly for the accounts manager. Your answer should be in the format of a typical computer-produced line-printer report.

(Chartered Association of Certified Accountants)

9   (a)   AB Chemicals Ltd is proposing to computerize its order processing and sales invoicing system. As the systems analyst working on this system, you are required to draft the invoice/advice note which will be printed out by the computer. Your draft design should provide for the computer to print out the following data fields:

- invoice address
- delivery address
- customer order no.
- ABC Ltd order no.
- customer account no.
- quotation no.
- sales district code
- sales representative's code
- invoice date
- product code
- product description
- quantity
- unit price
- total price for each product
- carriage and packing charge
- invoice total

Use a full page of your answer book to show your design of this document and state any assumptions you have made. Ignore VAT calculations.

(b)   In order to prepare a usable document, the systems analyst would need to obtain further information about the 16 data fields shown above. What would this further information consist of?

10   (a)   Prepare a checklist for the guidance of both O & M officers and systems analysts when designing forms for use in new procedures or systems.

(b)   Explain why good forms design is so important.

(Chartered Association of Certified Accountants)

11   (a)   Draft the systems flowchart for a computer-based payroll system.

(b) Provide notes to your flowchart, explaining the activity that is taking place at each stage of the system.

(Chartered Association of Certified Accountants)

12 A transactions file is to be processed so as to produce a report under defined analyses headings. At the same time a master file is also updated. The computer processing is done weekly, and a large proportion of the records on the master file are affected.

Draw a systems flowchart to show how the processing would be arranged, and briefly explain the reasons for your choice of backing storage.

13 A company receives orders from customers for goods which are sold direct from stock.

The order details when received are entered on to suitable source documents, which are batched and sent to the data processing department for keying to form file TI.

This file is then processed to update an outstanding order master file T2 held in delivery date sequence within customer.

Before entering details of goods required by customers on T2, a check is made against the customer master file MFI to ensure credit worthiness.

The updated master file T2 is then processed to produce details of orders to be delivered from stock. Orders to be delivered are removed from T2 and transferred to a daily deliveries file T3 which is subsequently used as input to the next day's invoicing and ledger update run.

Illustrate in the form of a systems flowchart the processing described.

Note: the master stock file is MF2 and no out-of-stock positions will arise.

14 (a) Draw a system flowchart showing the main programs which would typically be required in a computer-based stock control system.

(b) Give, and briefly explain:
- five examples of transaction or amendment data which would normally be input into such a system
- five examples of the kind of reports you would expect the system to produce, also indicating their frequency

(Chartered Association of Certified Accountants)

15 A manufacturing company employing approximately 2500 people uses a computer to deal with payroll accounting. The system is designed to meet the requirements of weekly and monthly paid employees.

Prior to the main weekly or monthly computer runs an employee master file (held on disk) is updated. There are about 200 transaction records giving details of changes to be made to the master file each week.

You are required to:

(a)   give five reasons for updating the master file;

(b)   name three outputs other than weekly and monthly payroll that could be produced from the computerised payroll systems;

(c)   draw a systems flowchart for the master file update.

16   The processing of data in batches typically commences with the origination of data and subsequently makes use of the following programs:

● validation program
● sort program
● master file update program

Draw a systems flowchart to show the stages in processing where the above programs would be used.

Your flowchart should include an indication of any other processing steps together with a brief explanation as to what is happening at each processing stage.

(Association of Accounting Technicians)

17   (a)   You are required to draw up a systems flowchart for the weekly wages routine of an organization's computer-based payroll system. The organization has a disk-based system with key-to-disk as the main form of batch data preparation. Your flowchart should be annotated as necessary.

(b)   Give the content layout of a single record in the employee file used in the above system.

(Chartered Association of Certified Accountants)

18   Describe in detail the checks and controls that can be applied to input data before it is used to update a master file.

Assume a batch processing system.

(Chartered Association of Certified Accountants)

19   Input validation runs are designed to eliminate the processing of incorrect data. The procedure involves writing a program which contains checks to be applied to all or some of the data fields which make up a record. Briefly describe ten checks that could be performed during a validation run.

20   Controls are invariably incorporated into the input, processing and output stages of a computer-based system.

(a)   State the guidelines which should normally be followed in determining what controls should be built into a system.

(b) Identify and briefly describe one type of control which might be used to detect each of the following input data errors:

● error of transcription resulting in an incorrect customer account code;

● quantity of raw material normally written in pounds weight but entered in error as tons;

● entry on a despatch note for a product to be despatched from a warehouse which does not stock that particular product;

● five digit product code used instead of a six digit salesman code;

● invalid expenditure code entered on an invoice.

(Chartered Association of Certified Accountants)

21 (a) Describe a general schematic diagram of a validation routine assuming a computer configuration that has key-to-disk input and magnetic disk storage.

(b) Describe *five* types of checks that are commonly used within a validation program.

(Chartered Association of Certified Accountants)

22 A system investigation usually produces a systems specification or systems definition.

(a) What are the main contents of a systems specification?

(b) What are its purposes?

(c) To whom is it directed?

(Institute of Cost and Management Accountants)

23 (a) Explain the reasons for preparing a fully detailed systems specification.

(b) Tabulate the essential contents of a systems specification.

(Chartered Association of Certified Accountants)

24 (a) Briefly summarise the main purposes served by a systems specification.

(b) Tabulate the main sections of a typical systems specification and give details of the principal contents of each section. You are to assume that a computer is already installed and that no further computing equipment will be required.

(Chartered Association of Certified Accountants)

25 Outline the main stages in the development of a systems project and briefly describe the work carried out by the systems analyst at each stage.

(Chartered Association of Certified Accountants)

20

Programming, implementing and maintaining the system

20.1 Programming

Once the systems specification has been approved by all interested parties, possibly after modifications have been made to it, the writing of the programs which will carry out the processing tasks within the system can begin.

For each program which the programmers will need to write, a **program specification** must be prepared by the analyst. Using the specifications as their terms of reference, as described fully in Chapter 14, the programmers then write and test the required programs.

During the program writing stage, the analyst will liaise closely with the programmers, in an attempt to clarify doubtful points, clear up ambiguities, and correct errors.

20.2 Systems testing

20.2.1 The role of systems testing

It is most important that computer systems do not contain errors. The systems testing phase is carried out in order that any errors remaining after programs have been individually tested can be detected and rectified. Systems testing should therefore:

1 further test the robustness of each program in the system;
2 test that all programs in a system are compatible one with another, so that a file output by an update program can be read by a print program, for example;
3 test that the computerized elements of the system interface successfully with the system's clerically-operated aspects.

20.2.2 The nature of systems testing

To test a newly-written system, dummy data which contains correct and invalid items should be used, and the expected results determined. The data must be carefully devised so that it checks the accuracy of each program. The following staff should be involved in the creation of the test data:

● the user department's staff
● the systems analyst
● the programmers
● the auditors

When testing a system, the following items will all need to be examined:

● details of all input files, both transactions and master files
● details of all output files
● printed reports from all stages of the processing
● screen displays

All output must be meticulously checked against anticipated results, to ensure that the system is behaving exactly as specified. Any discrepancies will need to be examined, so that the causes can be determined. Amendments will then need to be made to the program(s) and, in consequence, the documentation will have to be altered so that it reflects the changes.

When the systems analyst and his/her team are satisfied with the results of systems testing and believe that the system is robust, the process terminates.

20.2.3   The systems test

The test data used for systems testing should cover conditions such as the following:

1   range errors, for example in ages;
2   format errors, a digit in a surname, for example;
3   zero or negative values where only positive values are allowed; quantity ordered is an example;
4   non-integers in such fields as quantities;
5   a transaction record which is not matched by a corresponding master record;
6   a master record which is not matched by a transaction, or which is matched by more than one transaction;
7   invalid combinations of data; a sex code set to 'M' combined with a title set to 'Miss' for example.

In addition, controls should be rigorously tested, and the correction and re-submission of erroneous data should be carefully tried out.

20.3   Documenting the system

When the system is being tested, the analyst will usually be carrying out the task of bringing the system's documentation up-to-date. Accurate documentation is essential, so that implementation can be carried out and so that a system can be run on a day-to-day basis.
    The analyst should ensure that the following items are available when the system goes live;

1   an accurate and up-to-date systems specification;
2   accurate and up-to-date program specifications;
3   the current version of each source program listing;
4   the current version of each program flowchart;
5   test data and expected results.

In addition, the following documents will need to be prepared:

6   A clerical procedures manual   This document has the following functions:
(a)   It tells the staff of the user department how to run the system. To achieve this, it details the input which they will have to prepare

in order to carry out the various functions which the system has been designed to be capable of, and it details the output which the system produces.

(b) It acts as a training document, so that new members of staff can be easily assimilated into the user department.

(c) It acts as a reference document for the staff throughout the life of the system and, therefore, has to be constantly kept up-to-date.

(d) Because it establishes a uniform, standard approach to work in the user department, it makes for uniformity and consistency.

Its contents should include:

(a) a **summary** of the data processing system;

(b) an **outline** of the system in terms of the processing carried out, the files used, the output produced, and any security measures which need to be taken. A systems flowchart will be included;

(c) a **description** of each individual procedure in the system, saying when and by whom it needs to be performed, and what exactly is involved;

(d) the **documentation** which is used to input data to the system, showing how each form is to be completed, and what the maximum and minimum values in each field can be;

(e) the **output** which the system produces must be detailed, with examples of each report;

(f) where appropriate, the **dialogue** between the user and the system should be specified, so that staff are clear as to what is expected of them in a real-time environment;

(g) a list of errors and their meanings should be given, so that users are aware of the corrective action which should be taken when things go wrong;

(h) a glossary of terms is helpful, both computer terms and user jargon.

7 Operating instructions This document should tell the operations staff everything they need to know to run the system on an operational basis. It thus acts as a reference document during the life of the system, helps in the training of new staff, and enables a uniform and consistent approach to be established. An operations manual should contain the following sections:

(a) a **summary** of the data processing system;

(b) a **description** of the system in terms of the processing carried out, the files used, the output produced, and any security measures which need to be taken. A systems flowchart will be included;

(c) the computer **procedures** will be described in detail in terms of such factors as:

- memory size
- run-time
- setting-up procedures
- pre-printed stationery
- re-start procedures
- error messages and required action
- distribution of output

(d)   the **control** of the files used by the system will be detailed:

- taking security copies
- retention periods for back-up copies
- labels

8   Data preparation instructions   A guide should be prepared to assist the data preparation staff to carry out their jobs efficiently. Samples of input forms and any special requirements will be included.

In some computer installations, the functions of systems development and the maintenance of systems are separated. In such circumstances, the staff responsible for maintenance are often empowered to refuse to accept a new system whose documentation they believe to be unsatisfactory.

20.4   Staff training

20.4.1   The need for training

If the systems analyst has carefully involved the user department's management and staff in the processes of systems investigation and design, then they will be sympathetic to the analyst's new system at the implementation stage. And yet they will probably still be anxious and, possibly, resistant to change.

Staff training thus has several functions:

(a)   to convince the user department staff that the new system is an effective and efficient one;

(b)   to enable the staff to carry out the tasks required of them in support of the system;

(c)   to overcome their fear of change, and any feeling that they may not be able to cope with the demands of the new system.

20.4.2 Who should be trained?

The extent of the training which will need to be undertaken before a new system is implemented will depend on several factors, among them the amount of computer awareness existing in the organization, the complexity of the new system, and the calibre of the staff. Basically, however, all staff who will come into contact with the system will need some training. This will include:

(a) the management and staff of the department(s) whose work is being computerized;
(b) the staff of any other department which is at all affected by the new system;
(c) the organization's management;
(d) staff in the EDP department such as operators and data preparation staff;
(e) the auditors.

20.4.3 Methods of training

The following methods of training staff should be used as appropriate:

- lectures
- films
- group discussions
- case studies
- role playing
- literature

Clearly, those methods should be used in combination to achieve the best results. Where possible, actual practice in carrying out the new tasks should be given.

Careful thought will have to be given to the planning of the staff training.

20.5 The changeover

When a new system has been thoroughly tested and documented, and the staff who are affected by it have been trained, then the system can be implemented. This will involve two major aspects:

(a)   the changeover from the old system to the new one; and
(b)   the creation of a new file, either from scratch or by converting an existing file.

As these two issues are intimately interconnected, we will discuss them together in this section. Several different approaches can be made to the problem of changing over to a new system.

Straight changeover

Where a system is a small, relatively simple one, or where no other method appears viable, straight changeover may be opted for. In such a case the old system ceases to run one day, and the new system commences to run on the next. Such an approach presumes that a system has been completely tested and that the user department's staff have confidence in it. Clearly, the cost of a direct changeover will be low, but the risks involved, if something should go wrong, are considerable.

A straight changeover can be used in conjunction with one or other of the following methods of file creation:

1   **Straight file creation**, where the whole file is created immediately prior to the first run of the new system; this may be feasible where a small file is concerned.

2   **Dummy file creation** may be more helpful in other circumstances. Using this approach, for example in a payroll system, a master file would be set up containing a record for each employee. Each record could have standing data such as name, birthdate, tax-code and address entered into it many weeks before the planned changeover data, thus greatly spreading the workload over a longer time period. All that would need to be done immediately prior to the take-on of the new system is to add variable data such as pay-to-date, amend items that have changed since the records were created, add records for any new employees who have joined the organization, and delete the records pertaining to those who have left.

Pilot running

Where the volume of data involved in a system is too great to be coped with by a straight changeover, or where the establishments being dealt with are geographically scattered, a **pilot scheme** may be opted for.

Pilot running involves the gradual take-on of parts of a system one-at-a-time. A bank, for instance, could computerize one branch, then a second branch, and so on; an organization could gradually computerize each factory, depot or region, in order to spread the workload and to enable one team of specialists to carry out the implementation smoothly.

Pilot running lends itself to **phased file creation**, where parts of the master file are created or converted one-by-one. Of course, each part of the master file can be dealt with using straight or dummy creation methods, as appropriate.

Pilot running will only be suitable in the right circumstances but, where it can be used, it spreads the workload and reduces the risk of a disastrous failure at take-on time.

Parallel running
Where a computer system produces fairly similar output to that produced by the system which it is replacing, **parallel running** may be used. This implies that, when operation of the new system begins, the old system is left running.

In Fig 20.1, the new system begins operation in April but instead of dropping the old system after its March run, the old system is carried on for three months. During those months the output from the two systems is meticulously compared, to ensure that the new system is robust.

Parallel running is thus, in effect, an extension of systems testing. The cost of using this approach is very high, as the staff are asked to run two systems at once, but the method gives a good back-up because the manual system is continued for a time. It may well increase staff confidence in the new system, too, as the clerical staff can see for themselves that the new system 'works'.

Of course, straight or dummy file creation methods could be used in conjunction with parallel running.

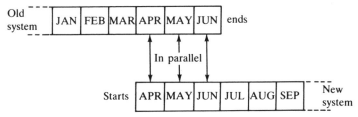

Fig 20.1   Parallel running

Other variations

It will be clear to the reader that the implementation methods outlined above are only summaries of some of the techniques which are often used during the take-on stage. In practice, the analyst and the user agree the most appropriate method of implementation for the particular circumstances they find themselves in. A combination of the above methods, such as a pilot scheme which involves the parallel running of each sub-system taken on, could be used. It may even be possible to compromise by first taking on only some of the procedures which will be performed by the total system, leaving the rest of the processing tasks to be carried out manually for the time being. Later the other procedures can be implemented. This is sometimes known as **partial** or **gradual conversion**.

20.6   The post-implementation review

However much effort a systems analyst spends on the investigation, design and development of a new system, there is always the chance that it does not exactly fit the user's needs. To ensure that no major factors have been overlooked, and to determine how closely the user's requirements have been met, a post-implementation review should be carried out.

The EDP team, the users and the auditors should meet after the system has been running operationally for a short time, and they should review the system in an attempt to ascertain how close its performance is to that which was predicted at the design stage.

The contents of the post-implementation review report should be:

1 A **summary** of the findings, emphasizing any areas where the system has been found to be unsatisfactory, and indicating the future action which should be taken.
2 A review of the system's **performance** in terms of such factors as computer time taken for runs, turnaround times for batch jobs submitted by users, error rates, volumes of data entering the system, and amount of clerical effort needed to support the system.
3 The effect of **changes** in the environment of the system, in the technology on which the system depends, or of the expectations of the users.
4 A **cost/benefit** review of the system, showing how the actual costs and benefits compare with the anticipated costs and benefits.

5   Recommendations as to how the system should be changed in order that any shortcomings can be rectified.

20.7   Maintenance

The systems analyst's work does not end when the system has been implemented. Throughout its life, a system has to be maintained, to ensure that it can continue to operate effectively and efficiently over time. For our purposes, two distinct types of maintenance can be identified as outlined below.

Emergency maintenance
Program testing and systems testing, however diligently they are carried out, can never guarantee the absence of bugs in a system. Clearly, in the first few cycles of operation, such bugs are likely to emerge and cause programs either to come to a sudden unexpected end, or to produce nonsensical results – garbage. Even after a program has been running for several months or years, it is possible that a unique combination of data will enter the system and cause a hitherto undetected bug to come to light.

Whenever such problems arise in the running of operational programs, they must be investigated and corrected immediately, so that the system involved can go back 'on stream' in order to produce the required information. The question of who should be responsible for the emergency maintenance of operational systems is dealt with in Unit 5, when the organization of the EDP department is discussed.

Modifications and development
Systems analysts try very hard to design flexibility into computer systems. But however well they manage to do this, a system will need to be modified or developed at some stage of its operational life. Changes may be required for one or more of the following reasons:

1   After a system has been running for a certain length of time, it may become clear to the DP personnel that its efficiency could be improved by carrying out certain tasks in a different way.
2   The user may require changes to the system, having had a chance to see how it actually works in practice. A change of personnel in the user department can often lead to such a request.

3 Changes may be required because the circumstances surrounding the system have altered; company policy may have changed, the organization's structure or the products it manufactures may have been modified, the volume of transactions may have grown, or other systems which impinge on the system in question may have been computerized.

4 New hardware or software may come onto the market which makes the 'old' way of doing things obsolete, and relatively costly.

5 Bodies or events external to the organization may cause changes to be required. The government, with legislation on such matters as taxation, is an obvious example.

Whatever cause gives rise to the need for changing an existing computer system, maintenance will have to be carried out. This will involve re-specifying parts of the affected program(s) and re-writing and re-testing them.

Clearly, the cost of carrying out the maintenance will depend, inter alia, on the quality of the documentation which accompanies the system.

Whenever changes are made to a system, all its documentation will have to be carefully revised and brought up-to-date.

20.8   Planning and monitoring a project

Because expensive resources are used to develop computerized systems, the work of those involved should be carefully **controlled**. This can be done by undertaking the following steps:

1 Each task which will need to be undertaken so that the system can be successfully developed needs to be identified.

2 The time to be taken for each task must be estimated in human working-days, and the estimates recorded on a project control form.

3 From the time estimates, estimates of costs can be drawn up.

4 Tasks can then be allocated to members of the project team.

5 As the system is developed, progress can be monitored against the estimates. This monitoring can take the form of monthly progress meetings where **time taken** plus **time still required** can be compared with **estimate** so that variances can be spotted, users informed and, where necessary, corrective action taken.

Where appropriate, such formalized control tools as critical path analysis (network charts) or Gantt charts (bar charts) can be used.

20.9 Summary

After a system specification for a new system has been approved, programs are written and tested. The new system can then be implemented. Throughout its life an operational system has to be maintained.

Examination questions

1 After the formal approval of a system specification, the next stage in a computer project is to implement the newly-designed system. An essential part of implementation is file conversion whereby a master file, typically held on a magnetic medium, is created.

Explain, with the aid of a flowchart, the activity of file conversion and indicate the importance of this work.

(Chartered Association of Certified Accountants)

2 Systems changeover and file conversion are two important stages in the implementation of a newly-designed computer system. Describe and comment on each of these activities.

(Chartered Association of Certified Accountants)

3 (a) What are the major tasks to be undertaken in systems analysis and design? (Your answer should be a concise explanation – excessive detail is not required.)

(b) As a method of systems changeover explain what is meant by parallel running and state its disadvantages.

4 An important decision to be taken with regard to the implementation of a system is the method of changeover to be adopted.

Describe the different methods of changeover available, and indicate the circumstances in which each would be appropriate.

(Chartered Association of Certified Accountants)

5 A stock control system has been developed to the stage where detailed specifications have been passed from the systems analyst to the chief programmer for program writing to commence.

Required:

(a) What additional work would the systems analyst have to do after passing specifications to the chief programmer and before the system becomes fully operational?

(b) Describe in detail how the stock master file would be converted for the new system; pay special attention to the methods that should be used to ensure that the file content is accurate.

(Chartered Association of Certified Accountants)

21

Structured systems analysis and design methodology (SSADM)

21.1 The nature of SSADM

Since the 1960s, when computers began to be widely used for the carrying out of business tasks, many surveys on 'user satisfaction' have been conducted. These surveys usually find great dissatisfaction among the users of computerized systems, perhaps because of the costs incurred, the time taken to develop the system, the difficulty of making even the smallest changes, the quality of the information produced, or any number of other factors.

One attempt among many to address this problem was the development of SSADM. Other structured methodologies exist. SSADM uses a standard approach in the analysis and design stages of the development of a computerized system, so that productivity can be increased and the quality of the resulting systems enhanced. SSADM encourages flexible systems design, it allows progress to be monitored as work is carried out, and it thus facilitates planning.

SSADM utilizes three sets of standards:

1 Structural standards which define a number of major stages, each consisting of a number of steps and tasks.
2 Procedural standards which relate to particular techniques: data flow diagrams are an example.

3   **Documentation standards** which define the forms and documents that are used throughout.

The outputs from an SSADM project are program specifications, file or database designs, the manual procedures required for the system to function, the operating instructions, and a plan of how the system will be implemented.

21.2   The tools used in SSADM

Various tools and techniques are used in SSADM. Before looking at SSADM in some detail, it may be helpful to review some of those tools.

21.3   Data flow diagrams (DFDs)

DFDs were dealt with in subsection 18.5.8. It may be helpful to review that section before reading on.

21.4   Logical data structures (LDS)

21.4.1   Entity modelling

Entities are the facts about which an organization, and therefore a system, holds data. A manufacturing company, for example, would consider products, suppliers, customers and employees as entities. The reason for looking at data in some detail is that, if we understand our data then we will have a better chance of designing efficient files and databases, and this will allow the cost-effective retrieval of data items to take place when required.

LDS is one method of **entity modelling**. For our purposes, an entity model is a diagrammatic representation of the entities used by a system and their relationships. For any one entity there will usually be many **entity occurrences**, corresponding to records in a file:

CODE	DESCRIPTION	COST	MATERIAL	FACTORY
123456	SCREW	0.05	BRASS	12
345678	BOLT	0.10	STEEL	34
456789	WASHER	0.02	BRASS	34

For each entity occurrence, there will be one or more attributes, data items or fields, such as code and description, above.

One attribute usually identifies the occurrence: this is often known as the key field, and 'code' is clearly the key in the above example.

An attribute of one entity may be the identifier of another entity: an example is 'factory', above, where that attribute is the key of the entity 'factory'.

LDS is concerned with the ways in which one entity is related to another entity, in terms of the organization using it.

We are interested in four relationships:

- one-to-one   (1 : 1)
- one-to-many   (1 : m)
- many-to-one   (m : 1)
- many-to-many   (m : n)

If a company has one managing director, and (s)he holds such a post in only one company, the relationship is one-to-one:

MD-company   1 : 1

If the company makes several differentiated products which no other organization manufactures, then it has a one-to-many relationship with its products:

company-product   1 : m

Where entity X and entity Y have a 1 : m relationship, then Y is the master and Y is the detail.

If many customers buy many products, then this relationship is many-to-many:

product-customer   m : n

When using LDS, each entity is shown as a named rectangle. Direct relationships are shown as straight lines. Where a 'many' relationship is involved, a 'crow's foot' is used, so that the relationships described above would be shown as follows.

One-to-one:

One to many:

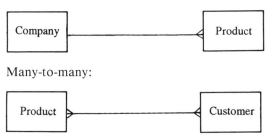

Many-to-many:

21.4.2 An LDS example

Let us see how LDS can be used in practice. Consider the following example.

A company has one chief executive officer, who is not employed by another company. The company has several divisions, each of which employs several people: no employee works for more than one division. Each division produces several products: no product is made by more than one division. Each product may be made out of one or more raw materials; any raw material may go into one or more products. Construct an LDS of the above.

The steps are:

1 The entities should be listed. In our example this produces:

- company
- CEO
- division
- employee
- product
- raw material

2 A relationship grid should be created which shows an X where one entity is directly related to another, as shown in Fig 21.1.
3 An initial diagram can then be constructed as shown in Fig 21.2.

21.4.3 Problems

The problem with Fig 21.2 is that many-to-many relationships are difficult to handle in most database systems. There are several

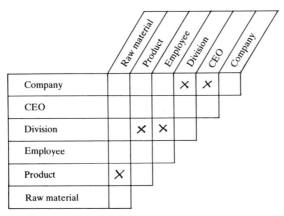

Fig 21.1   An LDS relationship grid

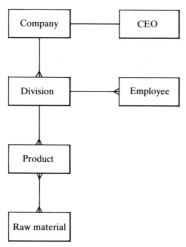

Fig 21.2   Initial logical data structure

reasons for this, but suffice it to say here that, if we wish to answer such questions as 'what products is material X used for?' or 'what materials go into product Y?', then this will be difficult to do without putting much product detail into each material record and/or putting much material detail into each product record. Either of these approaches would be repetitious and thus wasteful of storage and processing time, and would lead to variable length records, which many database systems do not allow.

A solution to this problem is to leave the original records unaltered, and create a file which relates the key fields of the products with the key fields of the associated materials:

PRODUCT   MATERIAL

123   XYZ
123   ABC
123   HJK
345   JKL
345   ABC
777   XYZ
777   BNM
777   ABC

We can now easily find the details of the materials in each product by first searching this file, and then enquiring of the relevant materials record(s).

This link file has, in effect allowed us to do away with the many-to-many relationship between product and material, and replace it with:

The link entity has a key which is a combination of the keys of the parent entities. In effect, the link entity is detail to both of the other entities. Our LDS now takes the form shown in Fig 21.3.

We shall examine the role of logical data structures later in this chapter.

21.5 Entity life histories (ELHs)

A thorough understanding of the operation of a system can only be gained by analysing it from a number of different viewpoints. Data flow diagrams show the processes in a system, while logical data structures look at the relationships between data items: but both are **static**.

An ELH, on the other hand, shows what happens to an entity as time passes. An ELH starts with the creation of an entity, records the changes which take place during its life, and ends when the entity leaves the system.

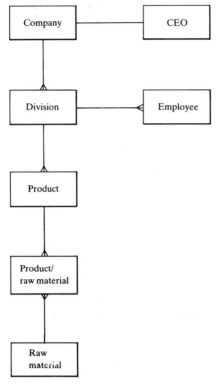

Fig 21.3 Final logical data structure

A much simplified ELH for a customer record is shown in Fig 21.4. Note that:

*   means repetition
o   means options

21.6 Relational data analysis (RDA)

21.6.1 The role of RDA

Relational data analysis complements entity modelling, by allowing us to check:

● that data is fully defined
● that all inter-dependencies have been identified

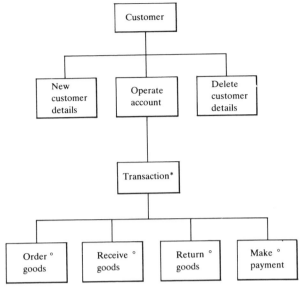

Fig 21.4   Entity life history

- that all ambiguities have been eliminated
- that there is no unnecessary duplication of data
- that data is optimally structured so that it will be able to support the different uses to which it will be put
- that cost-effective maintenance is possible

RDA allows us to reduce complicated masses of data into simplified and flexible record structures which can be used, for example, in a database system.

21.6.2   Entities and keys

We begin by furthering the discussion of entities and their keys which we undertook when we were dealing with logical data structures in Section 21.4.1, as an understanding of these topics plays an important part in understanding RDA.

In a payroll system, each employee is identified uniquely by an employee number: this is a **simple key**.

A college course consists of optional modules. Each student takes several modules and, of course, each module is taken by many students. A file could thus take the form:

STUDENT	MODULE			
123456	98765	......	......	......
123456	76543	......	......	......
234567	87654	......	......	......
345678	76543	......	......	......
456789	87654	......	......	......

No single key can uniquely identify a record, as both the students and the courses exist in their own right: each 'has a life of its own', so that students have names, and modules have descriptions. To access a particular record, we thus need to specify a **compound key** consisting of *both* student number *and* course number.

Where projects in a company consist of tasks, it may be convenient to number those tasks **sequentially**, starting from 1, for reference purposes. Thus:

PROJECT	TASK NO	DESCRPTN	COSTING	START
123456	1	ABC	123.56	NOV 95
123456	2	DEF	45.87	MAR 96
234567	1	XYZ	678.45	JAN 95
234567	2	VWX	9.76	MAY 95
234567	3	ABC	234.00	OCT 85

While it is therefore possible to ask about the total cost of project 234567, it is *not* possible to ask the starting date of task 2, *without* specifying the project number. This is because the tasks do not 'have a life of their own' outside the projects. To say project 234567/task 2 is to use a **composite key**.

21.6.3   Unnormalized data structures

Consider the following data, which is held by a college concerning each of its students. The conventions used are explained below.

STUDENT-DETAILS
    STUDENT-NUMBER
    NAME
    ADDRESS

DATE-OF-BIRTH
MODULE-LINE *
   MODULE-CODE
   TITLE
   TYPE
   DURATION
   DEPARTMENT
PREVIOUS-COLLEGE-LINE *
   COLLEGE-CODE
   NAME
   ADDRESS
   PHONE
   DATE-LEFT

Various conventions exist for describing data structures, but let us take the above to mean:

1 The structure called STUDENT-DETAILS consists of the fields: STUDENT-NUMBER, NAME, ADDRESS DATE-OF-BIRTH. The underlined field is the key field.
2 The asterisk tells us that the repeating group MODULE-LINE can occur as often as needed.
3 The group consists of the fields MODULE-CODE, TITLE, TYPE, DURATION and DEPARTMENT. Similar considerations apply to the PREVIOUS-COLLEGE-LINE repeating group.

As the reader will understand, the above method of holding data would lead to massive redundancy in a computer system: module titles would be held over and over again in thousands of student records, for example, as would the name and the address of another local college which many of the students had previously attended!

Let us now attempt to **normalize** the above data, remembering that, at every stage in normalization, each data structure must have its own key.

21.6.4 Normalization step 1 − remove any repeating groups

Any repeating groups are removed from the unnormalized structure and placed into their own structure. So that it can be accessed, the new structure must have a compound key consisting of the key of the main structure **plus** a key from the repeated group. (In **other** examples, a composite key would be used.) This gives us:

STUDENT-DETAILS
  STUDENT-NUMBER
  NAME
  ADDRESS
  DATE-OF-BIRTH

MODULE-LINE
  STUDENT-NUMBER
  MODULE-CODE
  TITLE
  TYPE
  DURATION
  DEPARTMENT

PREVIOUS-COLLEGE-LINE
  STUDENT-NUMBER
  COLLEGE-CODE
  NAME
  ADDRESS
  PHONE
  DATE-LEFT

The data is now in **first normal form** (1NF or FNF). All data structures are fixed-length.

21.6.5   Normalization step 2 − partial key dependencies

Each structure with a compound key (and only a compound key) is examined. Any fields which do not depend on the **whole** of the compound key are removed to their own structure.

Thus, in the module structure, the title of the module and the department which runs it are independent of the student's number. They can be removed. The same considerations apply to the college's name, address and phone number − but not to the date on which the student left.

This leaves us with:

STUDENT-DETAILS
<u>STUDENT-NUMBER</u>
NAME
ADDRESS
DATE-OF-BIRTH

MODULE-LINE
<u>STUDENT-NUMBER</u>
<u>MODULE-CODE</u>

PREVIOUS-COLLEGE-LINE
<u>STUDENT-NUMBER</u>
<u>COLLEGE-CODE</u>
DATE-LEFT

MODULE-DETAILS
<u>MODULE-CODE</u>
TITLE
TYPE
DURATION
DEPARTMENT

PREVIOUS-COLLEGE-DETAILS
<u>COLLEGE-CODE</u>
NAME
ADDRESS
PHONE

The data structures are now in **second normal form** (2NF or SNF) and much redundancy has been removed.

21.6.6   Normalization step 3 – non-key dependencies

This step is similar to step 2. Here any non-key fields which are dependent on other non-key fields are removed to their own structures.

Let us assume in the example which we have been using, that, for the sake of simplicity, the college only runs four types of module:

- HNC modules which last 40 hours
- HND modules which last 60 hours
- first degree modules which last 60 hours
- post-graduate degree modules which last 20 hours

It is thus clear that a module's duration depends wholly on the type of module as, if we know the type then we can derive the duration. The opposite is not true, however, as a 60 hour module can be one of two types!

We can thus remove module duration to its own structure, to arrive at:

STUDENT-DETAILS
    STUDENT-NUMBER
    NAME
    ADDRESS
    DATE-OF-BIRTH

MODULE-LINE
    STUDENT-NUMBER
    MODULE-CODE

PREVIOUS-COLLEGE-LINE
    STUDENT-NUMBER
    COLLEGE-CODE
    DATE-LEFT

MODULE-DETAILS
    MODULE-CODE
    TITLE
    TYPE
    DEPARTMENT

PREVIOUS-COLLEGE-DETAILS
    COLLEGE-CODE
    NAME
    ADDRESS
    PHONE

MODULE-TYPE-DETAILS
  <u>TYPE</u>
  DURATION

In effect, although it was not a key field in the original structure, the module type is the key to the duration. It is thus known as a **hidden key** or a **foreign key**. We are now in **third normal form** (3NF or TNF). The role of RDA in SSADM is discussed later in this chapter.

21.7 The stages of SSADM

Some descriptions of SSADM include the feasibility study stage, others do not. If the feasibility study is *not* to be included, then SSADM can be considered to consist of the following two phases, comprising six stages:

Phase 1 Systems analysis
Stage 1 Analysis of systems operations and current problems
      The current system is documented, and the problems noted.
Stage 2 Specification of requirements
      The analyst needs to know **what** is required, rather than **how** it will work.
Stage 3 Selection of technical options
      A system is selected, from all the possibilities, in terms of service, cost, benefits and the like.

Phase 2 Systems design
Stage 4 Data design
      The logical data structure is defined.
Stage 5 Process design
      Processes are defined in detail, in terms of how outputs are to be produced from inputs.
Stage 6 Physical design
      The logical design is converted into a physical design which will run on a particular computer. Program specifications are written, manual procedures are designed, operating instructions are prepared and the implementation of the system is planned.

Of course, it is not mandatory that the above stages are always carried out completely in the sequence laid down above. Implementation plans should be given some thought fairly early in the cycle of activities, for example.

21.8   The steps in SSADM

The reader should remember that it is beyond the scope of this text fully to describe SSADM, and that what follows only attempts to give an idea of SSADM for examination purposes, being subject to simplification and omission throughout.

You should, however, carefully note the structured and formalized approach which SSADM uses. The steps taken, and the products produced thereby, are listed in full, but only to give you a feel for the methodology: it is not necessary to commit everything to memory.

Phase 1   Systems analysis
Stage 1   Analysis of systems operations and current problems
STAGE 1   Step 110 INITIATE ANALYSIS

This step involves the investigation of the existing system. A high-level data flow diagram is produced. The entities which the system is to deal with are identified, and a **logical data structure** (LDS) is produced, which shows the relationships between those entities.

The scope of the project is agreed, as are the relevant users. An initial problems and requirements list is produced; this will be reviewed throughout the life of the project.

STAGE 1   STEP 120 INVESTIGATE CURRENT SYSTEM
More detailed investigation is carried out on the processes carried out by the system, and lower-level DFDs are produced. At the lowest level of processing, elementary function descriptions, in narrative form, are produced.

STAGE 1   STEP 125 INVESTIGATE SYSTEM DATA
          STRUCTURE
An entity description is produced for each entity on the logical data structure. The LDS may thus need revising.

STAGE 1   STEP 140 DEVELOP PROBLEMS/
          REQUIREMENTS LIST
The list begun in step 110 is revised and updated.

STAGE 1   STEP 150 REVIEW INVESTIGATION RESULTS

A quality-assurance review of the progress made to date is carried out, involving an examination of all the documentation produced so far.

Stage 2   Specification of requirements

STAGE 2   STEP 200 DEFINE LOGICAL SYSTEM

The physical data flow diagrams during stage 1 are used to produce logical DFDs which show **what** is to be done by the system.

STAGE 2   STEP 205 DEFINE SECURITY, CONTROL AND
                         AUDIT REQUIREMENTS

Such topics as access limitation, the effects of the Data Protection Act, back-up procedures and error handling are considered here.

STAGE 2   STEP 210 DEFINE AND CONSOLIDATE USER
                         REQUIREMENTS

The problems/requirements list produced in stage 1 is revised on the basis of work carried out in steps 200 and 205. A constraints list, concerning times, costs and limits to organizational change, may be produced.

STAGE 2   STEP 220 IDENTIFY AND SELECT FROM
                         BUSINESS SYSTEMS OPTIONS

A number, perhaps six or so, of **business systems options** (BSOs) is outlined and discussed with the users: these will consist of DFDs plus narrative. For the preferred two or three possibilities, the DFDs are expanded, and an outline cost/benefit profile is produced. One BSO is selected for development.

STAGE 2   STEP 230 DEFINE CHOSEN OPTION IN DETAIL

The chosen option's DFDs are expanded. The problems/requirements list is revised, as are the elementary function descriptions.

STAGE 2   STEP 240 CREATE REQUIRED DATA
                         STRUCTURE

The logical data structure of the chosen option is developed, as are its entity descriptions.

STAGE 2   STEP 250 INVESTIGATE DETAILED SYSTEM
                         LOGIC

An entity life history is produced for each entity dealt with in the chosen solution. This shows how an entity originates, how it is processed, and how, when completed, it leaves the system.

For each major event, a logical dialogue outline (LDO) is produced, showing the 'conversation' between the user and the computer. Screen formats are created. All other documentation is revised, as required, so as to produce a required system specification.

STAGE 2   STEP 260 REVIEW REQUIRED SYSTEM SPECIFICATION

The required system specification is reviewed with the users. Once this is agreed, the next stage can be carried out.

Stage 3   Selection of technical options
STAGE 3   STEP 310 CREATE TECHNICAL OPTIONS

The required system specification produced in stage 2 describes the chosen business system option in terms of **what** it will produce. This step involves the creation of perhaps six outline technical options, each of which shows a possible physical implementation of the system – **how** it will work. After discussion with the users, a shortlist of two or three options can be created. Each is specified in terms of its technical environment (hardware and software), functional description (batch/on-line/manual elements), impact analysis (operational changes), development and implementation plan, and cost/benefit analysis.

STAGE 3   STEP 320 USER SELECTS FROM TECHNICAL OPTIONS

One of the technical options is chosen.

STAGE 3   STEP 330 COMPLETE AND REVIEW REQUIRED SYSTEM SPECIFICATION

The required system specification is revised to reflect the chosen technical option.

STAGE 3   STEP 340 DEFINE DESIGN OBJECTIVES

Performance targets for the new system are defined, and a design objective specification produced.

Phase 2   Systems design
Stage 4   Data design

(Stage 4, dealing with data design, and stage 5, dealing with procedure design, are carried out in parallel, as they are inter-dependent. When both are complete, stage 6 can be tackled.)

STAGE 4 STEP 410 RELATIONAL DATA ANALYSIS
The inputs and outputs defined in stage 3 are analyzed so as to produce simplified, optimal data groupings. The technique of relational data analysis (RDA) is used. The process is also known as normalization or third normal form (TNF), and optimized TNF relationships are produced.

STAGE 4 STEP 420 CREATE DETAILED LOGICAL DATA
DESIGN
The results of the RDA performed in step 410 are combined with the LDS produced in stage 3 to produce a composite logical date design. DFDs will need to be modified.

Stage 5 Process design
STAGE 5 STEP 510 DEFINE LOGICAL ENQUIRY
PROCESSING
Each data retrieval carried out by the system will be defined in a **logical enquiry process outline** (LEPO). Output formats and logical dialogue outlines will have to be formalized.

STAGE 5 STEP 520 DEFINE LOGICAL UPDATE
PROCESSING
Each update carried out by the system will be defined in a **logical update process outline** (LUPO). The required system specification will be revised.

STAGE 5 STEP 530 VALIDATE AND REVIEW LOGICAL
DATA DESIGN
The revised required system specification is checked, and authorization to continue is obtained. This step ends the logical systems design.

Stage 6 Physical design
STAGE 6 STEP 610 CREATE 1ST CUT PHYSICAL DATA
DESIGN
An initial physical design for the system is produced, bearing in mind the software, perhaps a DBMS, which will be used. This is known as the '1st cut' physical data design.

STAGE 6   STEP 620 CREATE PROGRAM
                  SPECIFICATIONS
LUPOs and LEPOs are grouped functionally to form program
specifications.

STAGE 6   STEP 630 CREATE PERFORMANCE
                  PREDICTIONS AND TUNE DESIGN
Following on from the work carried out in steps 610 and 620, program performance is calculated and compared with the design
objectives laid down in stage 3. Design may need to be modified as
a result: so may the objectives, but only after consultation with the
users.

STAGE 6   STEP 640 CREATE FILE/DATABASE
                  DEFINITIONS
Detailed specifications of file and database structure are finalized.

STAGE 6   STEP 650 COMPLETE PROGRAM
                  SPECIFICATION
The program specifications are finalized. System run-charts are
produced.

STAGE 6   STEP 660 CREATE SYSTEM TEST PLAN
Test plans are produced.

STAGE 6   STEP 670 CREATE OPERATION
                  INSTRUCTIONS
The operating instructions for each program are produced.

STAGE 6   STEP 680 CREATE IMPLEMENTATION PHASE
                  PLANS
Methods of file creation or conversion are detailed. Implementation plans are defined.

STAGE 6   STEP 690 DEFINE MANUAL PROCEDURES
A user manual is produced.

21.9   Summary

1   SSADM uses the **top-down** approach. A broad overview, or

'helicopter view', of the system is taken first. This is then refined into progressively greater levels of detail. This method makes the development of a system manageable, as detail can be specified while keeping the wider context in mind.

2 The approach requires that one step leads on to the next, with increasing refinement throughout. Changes to earlier work may be needed as development proceeds.

3 The methodology forces the analyst to look repeatedly at the system from several different viewpoints. Errors ought thus to be highlighted.

4 The 'data-driven' approach of SSADM is claimed to make the inclusion of unwanted data or the omission of required data unlikely.

5 SSADM requires the completion of 'quality assurance' steps throughout the carrying out of a project. This should improve the quality of the delivered system.

Examination questions

1 What benefits are claimed for organizations which use SSADM?
2 What is entity modelling? Why is it used?
3 Explain the process of normalization and say why it is used.
4 What are the main stages in SSADM?
5 **Normalization exercise**

A company keeps a file of consultants. For each one, data such as the following is held:

NUMBER	NAME	PHONE	GRADE	RATE	MILEAGE
12345	SMITH	123-4567	2	45.00	1.00

EXPERTISE:

CODE	DESCRIPTION
ABC	MICROCOMPUTING
CDE	OFFICE AUTOMATION
DEF	TELECOMMUTING

The grades are related to rates and mileage allowances thus:

Grade	Rate	Mileage
I	30.00	0.50
I	35.00	0.75
2	40.00	0.90
2	45.00	1.00
3	50.00	1.10
3	55.00	1.20
3	60.00	1.25

You are required to put the above into:

- unnormalized form
- INF
- 2NF
- 3NF

6 Logical data structures exercise

Draw an LDS chart for the following. An organization has several subsidiary companies, which are not subsidiaries of any other organization. Some of the organization's directors are also directors of other organizations.

Each subsidiary has a number of employees, each of which works only for that subsidiary. Each factory is allocated to one subsidiary only. Because of the nature of their work, some employees work at more than one factory within a subsidiary.

Each factory makes a number of products, some of which, for ease of distribution, are made at various factories within a subsidiary.

Each product needs various raw materials, which are used in various products.

An individual customer buys any number of products.

22

Computer systems

22.1 Introduction

We have examined the work of the systems analyst in the last five chapters, and now have an understanding of the way in which computer systems are designed and developed.

As the reader will realize, each system is uniquely designed to meet the particular requirements of a given situation, and so no two systems are exactly alike. Yet broadly similar problems lead to broadly similar solutions, and computer personnel tend to assign labels to 'types of system' in an attempt to categorize them. While this can be a dangerous practice, as different labels in computer work often mean different things to different people, it can also be a useful tool of communication if carefully employed. For this reason, and because examiners have a habit of using such cat-egorizations and such labels, we conclude this unit by looking at some of the 'types of system' that an analyst can design and implement.

22.2 Batch processing

We have seen that batch processing implies the gathering together of all the transactions relating to a particular system in a particular period, so that they can be applied to the relevant master file(s) in one run. A batch processing system will thus produce its reports periodically.

The advantages of such an approach are outlined in what follows:

1   Batch processing is **appropriate** for many of the routine tasks, such as payroll or invoicing, which are undertaken in every business. Because all transactions are batched together and applied to the master file(s) in one pass, the average cost of processing each transaction will be low.

2   Because the raw data is input in one or more batches, it is easy to **control.** As described in Chapter 19, trailer records containing counts and totals can be input with the data so that the computer can check the accuracy of the input.

3   When updating by copying is used, as it often is in a batch processing system, a new version of the master file(s) is automatically created. This makes the system more **secure**, as back-up is thereby created.

On the other hand, the batch processing approach does give rise to several problems and difficulties:

1   Reports are only produced **once per period**. It is not possible to interrogate the system as and when queries arise, because the system is 'time-driven'. While this will not matter in the case of a payroll system, it will be a crucial consideration in many other situations.

2   When reports are produced by a batch system, the data in them is already **out-of-date**. The system, at best, will report on the situation as it was when the data for the update run was collected. The time taken to prepare the data, verify it, validate it, update the file(s) and distribute the output will mean that inaccuracies will inevitably creep in.

3   Because the update run happens cyclically, **peaks** of work will occur in the department(s) responsible for inputting raw data to the periodic run and dealing with its output. This may, in extreme circumstances, lead to staffing problems.

4   Information may **not** be as **concise** as possible. Someone has to decide, in advance, what reports are needed to satisfy a particular need, and then design a system to produce those reports. Not all the information will be needed in practice each time. In extreme circumstances, such a computerized system may merely be a cheaper way of producing unnecessary information!

5   Conversely, information may be **incomplete** if exceptional

requirements are called for in a processing cycle. Only expensive changes to the batch processing system can remedy these faults.

22.3 Real-time systems

We have seen that real-time systems, unlike batch processing systems, are 'event driven' or 'transaction driven'. This means that enquiries can be made of the system, and transactions can be applied to it, at any time during the hours that the system is on-line. For this reason, such systems are also called interrogative, interactive, conversational and enquiry-response, systems.

1 As transactions or enquiries can be input to the system **on demand**, no rigidity is imposed upon the user of a real-time system.
2 'Instant' information can be retrieved from the system. This **speed of response** will be crucial in a banking system, a reservation system, or in certain stock control systems, for example.
3 When answers are output by the system, they will be completely **up-to-date**, reflecting the current situation.
4 If data transmission facilities are used in conjunction with a real-time processing system, as they often are, then establishments which are geographically **remote** from the central computer may reap the benefits of instantly-available, up-to-date information.

The problems and difficulties associated with the use of real-time systems on main-frame computers are:

1 Real-time systems are **costly**. This is because the following facilities are needed:

● software which is capable of handling transactions and enquiries in a real-time environment
● a large store to hold such software
● data transmission links between the computer and the terminals, if transactions and enquiries are to be made from remote establishments

2 Batch control records cannot be used in a one-off situation, and updating-in-place is less secure than updating-by-copying. This means that real-time systems are **less secure** than batch processing systems unless steps are deliberately taken to deal with this problem. Logging and dumping are possible solutions, but they do, of course, cost money.

3 When a user has gone over to a real-time system which carries out much of the data processing, (s)he is **vulnerable** to a failure in that system. In extreme cases, a standby system will have to be provided in case of a disastrous hardware or software failure.
4 Such systems are difficult to audit because many users, often at remote points, may have access to the system's files.

22.4   Database systems on main-frame machines

22.4.1   Problems with the traditional approach

The systems that we have been discussing in this chapter are systems which are essentially organized according to areas of work, perhaps departments in an organization. Each system has its own master file(s) and its own programs, and each accepts input and produces output independently of any other system. While such systems may be appropriate in many circumstances, they do have several potential disadvantages:

1 Data may well be **defined** and **classified differently** for different systems; an employee, for example, may be classified in different ways on the personnel, payroll and pensions files. This may lead to problems if information about that person is required from two different files.
2 The approach leads to **duplication of processing**. In the example given above, if the details regarding an employee should alter, then the new items of data will have to be input separately to the three systems, and three updating processes will have to be gone through.
3 **Data is duplicated** on the files. Not only is this wasteful, but it can lead to the further problem of **inconsistency**, where different values are input to and held on the different files.
4 **Back-up** files will also hold much duplicated data.
5 The processing systems are **not sufficiently broad** to aid management decision making as much as they might, because they each concentrate on one application.

22.4.2   The database approach

The use of a database attempts to overcome these problems. A database is a centrally-located, consolidated file which holds the data relating either to the whole of an organization's operations or the data relating to a major operational area. Databases are known also as data banks; they utilize the concept of the integrated file. Each application or system now no longer has its own file; instead, each system uses the same common database. Each item is held once only, needs updating once only when it changes, and can be retrieved as required. Access can be made to the database, which is held on a direct access storage medium, using remote terminals. The advantages of this approach to systems design can be said to be:

1 The system is **broader**. This means that there is less rigidity so far as its users are concerned. Information about any aspect of an application area can be accessed by management, as and when required, and up-to-date answers will be forthcoming.

2 Management can therefore **react more quickly** and in a **better informed** manner when a decision needs to be made, because a system which is broad in scope allows even ill-informed users to browse through the data base so that their ill-structured queries can be answered in an interactive fashion.

3 **Resources** are used more efficiently because there is less duplication all round; only one transaction is needed when an event takes place, and that transaction is then able to navigate to several areas of the database.

4 **Control** is facilitated; checks can be built into the database system in an attempt to ensure that only correct data is used for updating.

5 The **inconsistencies** which are inherent in the traditional approach are, to a large extent, eliminated by the use of the database.

6 The data items are **independent** of the programs which use them – only the software which looks after the database needs to be changed if the characteristics of a data item change, not every program which accesses that data item.

7 Because data items are arranged logically in the database, individual data items can be more easily found and overall access times are lowered.

8 When data is held in a central database with the proper control procedures, then **security** should be enhanced, as only authorized users will be allowed access to the data.

9 The work of **auditing** the system should be eased.

22.4.3   Using a database

A database will perhaps be created and used for each major application area in an organization; for example a database in the personnel area may combine the data previously held in the personnel, payroll and pensions systems' master files, or a single database may cover the design, purchasing, production, stock control and accounting functions in a manufacturing company. So that enquiries can be made of the database as and when required, it will have to be held on a direct access storage medium. To enable this to happen, a common system of classifying and coding the data will have to be agreed between the users of the existing systems.

In addition to the database, software will be required which handles the data in the database. This tends to be referred to by several names, among them **database management system** (DBMS), **database system** and **data management software**. The software is in effect an extension to the operating system, and it acts as an interface between the programs which need to access data in the database and the database itself, allowing the data to be retrieved or updated.

The way in which a particular DBMS works will, of course, depend on the way it has been written, but all such systems attempt to allow efficient access to be made to data.

In order to set up a database, the following steps need to be taken:

1   The needs of the users of the database need to be established.
2   The data items which the database is to hold can then be determined, and these can be defined. It is important to realize that the definition of the items is thus part of the DBMS, not part of the programs which access the data. All of the data items are known collectively as the **schema**.
3   The needs of individual users can then be defined in a **subschema**. Each user thus has an individual 'user view' of the database.
4   The appropriate database software is acquired. Programs can then be written which define the data in terms of the sub-schema relevant to the particular user − the DBMS links the program to the actual data.

22.4.4 The components of a DBMS

A **data definition language** (DDL) allows the database to be
defined, thus facilitating the setting up and subsequent maintenance of the database. The data items to be used, and the relationships between them are described, so that the system knows the
structure of records and files.

A **data manipulation language** (DML), known also as a query
language, allows information to be rapidly retrieved from the database. A typical query could take the form:

PRINT Number, Name, Department, Salary
    FROM Payroll-file
    WHERE Grade > 7 AND Sex = "F"
    SORT BY Name

A DML is often unique to a particular package, but the **structured
query language** (SQL) is a standard DML which is built into several
database systems. Other examples of query languages are QBE
(query by example) and QUEL (query language).

In many systems, it is possible to use a DML in conjunction with
a third generation language such as Cobol.

An application generator allows applications to be created
without the use of individual program statements, which are sometimes difficult to remember, and can easily be misused. A menu-
driven approach, along with the filling in of forms to show the
layout of screens and the like, is used. Customized applications are
thus built from ready-made program modules.

A report generator allows the format and layout of reports to be
defined. Headings and totals are described. Use of a report generator takes more time than use of a query language, but the user can
readily produce well laid-out and complex reports by this method.

Query languages, application generators, and report generators
can be considered as fourth generation languages (*see* Chapter 14)
as they are non-procedural, allowing a user to manipulate a database without worrying about *how* the task is to be accomplished.

A **data dictionary** (DD) is an item of software which defines the
data used by the system. Data items are named and described,
and validation checks specified. Any codes which are used for
individual items of data are defined. Access limitations are also

specified. The database administrator is responsible for the maintenance of the DD.

Database utilities allow 'housekeeping' routines such as the creation and deletion of records to be carried out.

22.4.5 Database types

1 Relational databases are widely used on all types of computers. They consist of a number of two-dimensional tables, or 'flat files', which can be linked or **related**, one to another, using key fields. Once normalization has been carried out (*see* Chapter 21) this leads to a very flexible approach.

2 A **hierarchical database** is like a branching tree with the root **node** at the top. Each level down the database has an increasing level of detail. An example is a company database which is divided into divisions, departments, sections, employees, and then into the attributes of those individual employees. Each **parent** segment can have many **child** segments, but each child has only one parent. This is thus a one-to-many relationship.

Structured requests which naturally 'come down' the hierarchy can be rapidly handled using this approach, but other retrievals may not be handled so efficiently as long searches may be needed. IMS/VS is a hierarchical database.

3 A **network database** permits a child to have more than one parent. Such a structure is called a plex structure. There are more inter-connections between data items than in the hierarchical approach, thus allowing more complex relationships to be defined. **Pointers** are used to relate one data item to others, so that retrievals can take place, but, of course, these connections are limited to the ones which have been designed into the system. A **chain** is a string of records joined by pointers. Such a system will be more memory-hungry than the equivalent hierarchical system. IDMS is a network database.

Network and hierarchical systems are simple to implement and, because the links are built into the system, their operation is fast and efficient. **All** the possible links cannot be built into the system, however, and so some operations cannot be carried out, or can only be carried out in an inefficient manner. Mundane day-to-day operations, which often utilize a hierarchy or network of relationships, can thus readily be carried out using such systems: if the operation of the system reveals that any required links have been omitted, then they can be inserted subsequently.

Relational databases may be less efficient than hierarchical or network systems, but they are more **flexible**, as the paths between data items do not need to be pre-defined. Relational databases thus lend themselves better to managerial and professional information systems, where requirements are ad hoc and unpredictable, and where departmental and file boundaries tend to be cut across. Many systems, of course, attempt to combine the best of both systems, by providing a network structure along with a relational interface for a management information system or an executive information system. The falling cost of memory facilitates such an approach.

22.4.6 The database administrator (DBA)

A member of staff known as the database administrator is responsible for:

1 The design and maintenance of the database, and the integration of new applications into the database.
2 Ensuring that the database documentation is kept up-to-date, and that the database is used in a standardized manner.
3 Supervising the recovery procedures after there has been a failure of the database.
4 Monitoring the performance of the database systems, and testing them as necessary.
5 Monitoring the control and security aspects of the operation of the database.
6 Controlling the usage of the database and, as required, reconciling conflicts between users.

22.4.7 The problems and difficulties

The database approach outlined above does pose problems and create difficulties which are not encountered when more conventional systems are in use. They are:

1 The **complexity** of such systems creates planning and co-ordination difficulties, and means that the time taken to investigate, design and implement such systems will be greater. Costs, of course, are higher too, and many organizations are unwilling to spend large sums of money on such systems, not knowing what the

benefits will be, when savings can still be made by implementing conventional systems.

2   The integrated nature of such systems means that they often cut across traditional **departmental boundaries**. This can lead to much resistance.

3   Such systems are difficult to thoroughly **test**.

4   **Security** problems arise; how is unauthorized access to be prevented?

5   **Back-up** needs to be carefully considered, too.

6   **Flexibility** is a problem. How can a complex database system be designed so that it can be altered when circumstances change? How can a system be structured so that it meets the needs of all users, at all levels?

22.4.8   Integrated data processing

The database approach implies a measure of integration; files which could be single entities are combined into an integrated whole which attempts to satisfy all users in a major application area of the organization's operations.

The use of phrases like 'integrated data processing' or 'the total system approach', however, often implies more than just the use of a database. Such terminology may indicate the use of large data banks containing all the internal and external information, about past, present and forecasted future events, which is needed by an organization. Such a design philosophy employs the systems approach, treating the whole organization as the system. Whenever such terms are used, careful definitions are called for.

22.5   Expert systems

22.5.1   The nature of expert systems

Artificial intelligence (AI) is an inter-disciplinary sub-field of computer science. It is concerned with the symbolic representation of knowledge and the way in which inferences can be made from that knowledge. AI is thus concerned with attempts to make computers act 'more like humans', and AI includes decision-making systems, robotics, natural language processing and others.

AI is a research field concerned with problem-solving in the abstract but, in the past few years, there has been a shift towards the creation of systems which contain huge amounts of specific knowledge about a particular problem: this is the aim of the 'expert system'.

A collection of AI techniques which attempts to assist humans in the analysis of problems and in decision-making in such areas as planning and scheduling, the diagnosis of disease, the location of mineral deposits, the elucidation of chemical structures, the diagnosis of ailments in engines, the monitoring of chemical plants and nuclear reactors – and other tasks – is known as **expert systems**, **knowledge-based systems**, or simply **knowledge systems**. It is the knowledge engineer who builds such systems.

A knowledge system uses:

1 A database of knowledge which is widely shared by human experts in the given field. This is often referred to as the knowledge base. The quality of performance of an expert system depends, in part, upon the size and quality of its knowledge base.
2 A knowledge acquisition module, which allows the system to 'learn' about the problem area or domain.
3 An inference engine, which allows the system to make deductions, and thus draw conclusions, from the data in its knowledge base.
4 A user interface, which allows the human user of the system to enquire of it and to input new knowledge.

Knowledge systems are now in use in many commercial organizations. They are, however, in their infancy and are at present limited to well defined, fairly narrow, tasks and cannot reason broadly over a large field.

22.5.2 Types of expert system

1 Expert systems can be written ab initio in languages such as **Prolog** (programming in logic) or **Lisp** (list processing).
2 A system can be built using an expert system shell which allows the user to build up the rules relating to a particular area.
3 Another type of shell, a rule-inducing shell, allows examples of previous decisions to be input to the system, so that it can infer its own rules from what has been decided in the past.

22.5.3 Prolog

We shall take a brief look at a simple knowledge system written in Prolog. Prolog uses controlled logical deduction. We give it the facts as we know them, and then ask whether or not a specific conclusion can or cannot be drawn from those facts. The knowledge engineer would thus say that Prolog's control structure is logical inference.

Languages such as Basic and Cobol require the programmer to tell the computer, in sequence, every step which it must make to carry out a given task. This **how** approach could be called the **procedural** approach.

Prolog, on the other hand, requires the user to describe the task in hand as a series of constraints which have to be satisfied. The user merely specifies **what** − it is the system which determines **how** the task is to be carried out when this **declarative** approach is in use. Some authorities regard languages such as Prolog as fifth-generation languages, but terminology in this area is very confused, and so such terms must be used with great care.

Of course, the declarative approach takes up more computer resources but, as the cost of hardware approximately halves every three or four years, this consideration is less important than the cost-effective use of expensive human resources. It is said that a Prolog program typically requires ten times fewer lines than the equivalent Pascal program.

Prolog is an important AI tool and is widely used in the development of knowledge systems. The Japanese chose Prolog as the fundamental language for their fifth-generation project. Because Prolog requires a user to make a well-structured description of a problem, it can also be used as a specification tool.

Consider the following Prolog program, and the notes which follow it:

```
/* PRO1 */
domains
        person, activity = symbol
predicates
        likes(person, activity)
        dislikes(person, activity)
clauses
        likes(adam, cricket).
        likes(adam, football).
        likes(bill, tennis).
        likes(cath, cricket).
        likes(cath, tennis).
```

```
likes(mary, X) if dislikes(adam, X).
dislikes(adam, tennis).
dislikes(bill, cricket).
dislikes(bill, football).
dislikes(john, X) if likes(adam, X).
```

The program statements mean the following:

The first line is a comment (starting with /∗ and ending with ∗/) which, in this case, names the program for future reference. Comments should be used wherever they are useful, and are completely ignored by the Prolog compiler.

The first two sections state that the relationship 'likes' involves two objects, both of which are character format, with a lower-case letter as the first character. A similar statement is made about the relationship 'dislikes'.

The clause 'likes(adam, cricket)' means, taking the first two sections into account, that the person 'adam' likes the activity cricket. The clause 'likes(mary, X) if dislikes(adam, X)' means that 'mary' likes any activity which 'adam' dislikes. X is a variable which denotes an unknown activity. In this version of Prolog, so that the system can differentiate between an object and a variable, variables must start with an upper-case letter.

The program would allow the user to type in such queries as:

```
likes(bill, tennis);
likes(X, cricket) which means 'who likes cricket?';
likes(cath, X) which means 'what activity does cath like?';
dislikes(X, Y) which means 'who dislikes what?';
likes (cath, X) and dislikes(adam, X) which means 'what
    does cath like which adam dislikes?'.
```

As the reader will appreciate from this simple example, it is possible to craft large, complex knowledge systems in Prolog, but the process is time-consuming and costly.

22.5.4 An expert system shell

An **expert system shell**, known also as an **expert system builder**, allows rules to be readily input to the expert system. For example, a major rule could be:

CREDIT IS ALLOWED IF
    INCOME IS SATISFACTORY
    OR SAVINGS ARE ADEQUATE
    OR A GUARANTOR IS AVAILABLE.

This could be broken down into sub-rules:

INCOME IS SATISFACTORY IF
    SALARY IS > £10 000 PER ANNUM
    AND THE JOB HAS BEEN HELD FOR > 3 YEARS.
SAVINGS ARE ADEQUATE IF
    BANK ACCOUNT IS > £5000
    OR SHARE PORTFOLIO > £7500

and so on.

When the system is run, the user is asked questions until the system is able to draw the correct conclusion. In the above example, if the answers to the questions 'Is Salary > £10 000?' and 'Has the job been held for > 3 years?' are both 'Yes', then the system would advise that credit is to be allowed, as this deduction can safely be made. Only if the answer to either of these questions were 'No' would questions relating to savings be asked.

Any number of levels of rules can be built up, and a user-friendly interface can readily be created using such systems. Crystal is a popular ES shell.

22.5.5   Rule-inducing systems

A problem with the shells discussed in the previous section is that the user has to know **how** decisions are made. This is not always the case in complex decision-making situations, where judgement and subjective considerations are applied. A rule-inducing system attempts to overcome this by allowing us to enter **previous decisions** into its knowledge base. The shell then induces the rules itself from the examples.

Thus, if the following examples concerning credit decisions were entered into the system:

SALARY	SAVINGS	CHILDREN	RESULT
25 000	0	9	ACCEPT
24 999	5000	8	ACCEPT
24 999	4999	6	REJECT
24 999	4999	5	ACCEPT

then the system would be able to induce the following rules:

IF SALARY IS AT LEAST 25 000
  THEN REQUEST IS ACCEPTED (REGARDLESS OF
  OTHER FACTORS)
IF SALARY IS < £25 000
  THEN IF SAVINGS ARE AT LEAST £5000
    THEN REQUEST IS ACCEPTED
IF SALARY IS < £25 000 AND SAVINGS ARE < £5000
  THEN IF CHILDREN < 6
    ACCEPT
  ELSE
    REJECT.

Where clashes exist in the examples, or where insufficient examples are available for a decision to be reached, the shell informs the user, so that corrective action can be taken. XPERT-RULE is an example of a rule-inducing shell.

22.6 Other types of system

Examination questions are asked concerning various 'types of system'. The following were discussed in Chapter 8 of Volume 1:

● local area networks
● wide area networks
● distributed data processing
● timesharing
● electronic data interchange
● electronic funds transfer
● value added networks

In addition, the electronic office, along with the software used therein, was discussed. Those sections should now be reviewed.

22.7   Systems theory

22.7.1   The nature of systems theory

A system is a set of inter-related elements which carries out a given task. Systems theory is the body of knowledge which allows systems to be studied, so that the behaviour of complex systems can be explained and, in certain circumstances, predicted.

A business systems accepts inputs, works upon them according to some pre-defined processing rules and produces outputs (see Fig 22.1).

So that a system can function in a controlled manner, there must be **feedback**. This means that, after processing has taken place, the results of that processing are fed back to an element of the system which is able to influence its behaviour, so that corrective action can be taken. Examples of systems which employ the principle of feedback are a heating system which uses a thermostat and an engine which is controlled by a governor. These are known as **closed loop** systems, and such a system is shown in Fig 22.2.

The following points should be carefully noted:

1 Inputs are processed according to the pre-defined rules which govern the operation of the system.

2 The **comparator** then compares the **output** with the standards which have been laid down. In a manual system this could be a clerk checking to see whether a product has fallen below its re-order level, or whether a customer has gone over the credit limit. In other circumstances, the function could be carried out by computer software.

3 Once the comparator has identified the variances, then the **effector** is informed of them, so that corrective action can be taken. This is done by adjustments being made to the inputs, the processing and, where necessary, the standards themselves. In a business environment, the manager is likely to be the one who determines the appropriate corrective action in a given set of circumstances; the manager is thus acting as the effector.

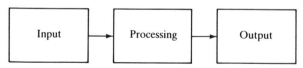

Fig 22.1   A business system

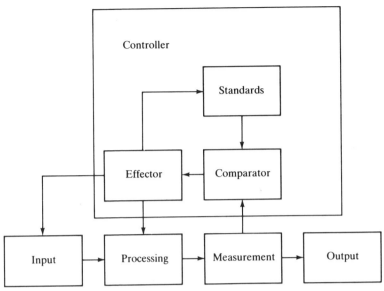

Fig 22.2   A closed-loop system

4 As shown in Fig 22.2, the comparator and the effector are collectively known as the **controller**.
5 Where there is no feedback, and so no measure of performance against standards, then an **open-loop** system is in use.

22.7.2 Positive and negative feedback

A negative feedback system works on the principle of trying to reduce the fluctuations around a standard or norm. In such a case, deviations are detected, and action is then taken in the opposite direction so that the deviations are eliminated. An example could be a company which decides to increase the working hours spent during a period because production has fallen below the target.

Positive feedback, on the other hand, is an attempt to amplify a detected deviation in order to increase efficiency. An example is a company which finds that it is spending more than it has budgeted for on sales, but also finds that its sales have, in consequence, gone up more than proportionally. In such a case, it may be in the interests of the company to further increase expenditure on sales.

22.7.3   Sub-optimization

Sub-optimization occurs when the objectives of one element, or sub-system, within the total system conflict with the objectives of the overall system. An example is when a marketing department prevails upon a credit control section to slacken the rigorousness of its credit control procedures. In such a case, the marketing department will probably achieve higher sales and it will, therefore, be more likely to achieve its own objectives. The company as a whole will suffer, however, as the losses through bad debts will increase also. Clearly, the sub-optimization has benefited one element of the system, but damaged the system as a whole.

Other examples could involve less demanding inspection, or more lax supervision.

22.7.4   Types of system

There are various ways of classifying systems:

1   Open and closed systems   An open system interacts with its environment. A closed system is independent of its environment, and does not interact with it. All business systems are, of necessity, open systems.

2   Open-loop and closed-loop systems   A closed-loop system uses feedback to control the performance of the system: a heating system with a thermostat is an example. An open-loop system relies on external control, which is not part of the system itself.

3   Deterministic,   probabilistic   and   cybernetic   systems
(a)   **Deterministic** (or **mechanistic**) systems are those where the end product is known exactly from the inputs. If a machine is working correctly, for example, then it may be possible to know beforehand what the precise outputs from an operation will be.
(b)   **Probabilistic** (or **stochastic**) systems only allow their outputs to be predicted within certain limits − their precise outputs cannot be known in advance because of the number of unquantifiable factors which affect them. Because of the nature of the business world, most commercial systems fit into this category.
(c)   **Cybernetic** (or **self-organizing** or **adaptive**) systems adapt to their environments. Humans, plants and organizations are examples of cybernetic systems. In order to survive in a competitive world, they must react; if they do not react, then they die.

4   Hard and soft systems   An automated production plant, where there are clear objectives, rigid rules and objective measures of performance, is a hard system. Soft systems are those concerned with human situations, where decision-making is carried out in a more uncertain environment.

22.7.5 Systems theory in practice

A study of control systems and systems theory is useful because:

1 It provides a theoretical framework which allows the performance of a business to be studied.

2 It stresses the fact that all organizations are made up of subsystems which must work together harmoniously in order that the goals of the overall system can be achieved.

3 It recognizes the fact that conflicts can arise within a system, and that such conflicts can lead to sub-optimization and, ultimately, can even mean that an organization does not achieve its goals.

4 It allows the individual to recognize that (s)he is a sub-system within a larger system, and that the considerations in the previous paragraphs apply to him/her, also.

5 Given the above factors, it is clear that information-producing systems must be designed to support the goals of the total system, and that this must be borne in mind throughout their development.

Questions

1 (a) What is meant by 'real-time processing'?
(b) Explain the hardware and software facilities which are required for the operation of a real-time system.
(Chartered Association of Certified Accountants)
2 (a) What are the characteristics of a real-time processing system?
(b) Give the advantages and disadvantages of a real-time system together with two examples of such a system.
(Chartered Association of Certified Accountants)
3 A large manufacturing company is contemplating the installation of a computer-based interrogation system for use by top management and some functional specialists, notably the financial and management accountants.

(a) Explain the general features of interrogation systems and how they would be of service to users.

(b) What are the major hardware and system design features necessary for an interrogation system to operate effectively?

(Institute of Cost and Management Accountants)

4 (a) Explain the term 'database' and how the operation of a data processing system using a database differs from one using conventional file structures.

(b) What advantages are to be gained from using a database system?

(c) What are the essential design features which should be incorporated into the system?

(Institute of Cost and Management Accountants)

5 Describe the organization of a typical database system paying particular attention to its hardware, software and administrative features.

(Chartered Association of Certified Accountants)

6 (a) Define the term 'systems theory', and explain why it is important for the accountant to understand the principal features of 'systems theory'.

(b) Briefly explain the meaning of each of the following terms:
● feedback
● open-loop system

(Chartered Association of Certified Accountants)

7 Explain the major features and mode of operation of a control system.

Your answer should, by way of illustration, make use of practical examples and diagrams as appropriate.

(Chartered Association of Certified Accountants)

8 What is an expert system? How do such systems arrive at decisions? In what areas are they used?

Unit Five
The installation and the industry

23

The data processing department

23.1 Introduction

In the last three units, we have seen what a computer is, how a computer is programmed, and how computerized systems are developed and put into operational use. In so doing we have come across some of the personnel who work in typical computer installations, and some of the organizations which are involved with computerized data processing. In this unit we look more fully at these two important topics. This chapter examines the job functions of the staff who are employed in a typical main-frame computer department and suggests ways in which such a department might be organized and run. Chapter 24 reviews the computer industry.

23.2 Data processing personnel

23.2.1 The data processing manager

Many computer installations are headed by a data processing manager who is responsible for the systems and programming work undertaken in the organization, and for the operation of the computer.

The data processing manager, like all managers, will carry out the functions of planning, organizing, directing, motivating, co-ordinating and controlling in the department. In addition to the usual management skills, an up-to-date knowledge of the technical aspects of computing will be needed; for this reason, most data processing managers have had experience in the fields of programming and systems analysis. Special responsibilities faced by the DPM are found in the areas of staffing, work standards and user relations.

Clearly, the precise role of the data processing manager will vary from one organization to another; much depends upon the size of the computer department.

23.2.2   The systems analyst

We saw in Unit 4 that the systems analyst is responsible for developing and testing computerized systems and then for implementing and maintaining them. To carry out these tasks an understanding of 'the computer' as an answer to data processing problems is necessary, as well as a knowledge of the capabilities and limitations of the particular computer configuration with which the analyst is working. In addition, the analyst requires a good deal of business knowledge and must be aware of the peculiarities of the specific organization for whom (s)he is working, in terms of its goals, the personnel employed by it, the products or services sold, the environment within which it exists, and any other relevant details.

Because of the initial resistance with which computerization is often met, the analyst must also be able to secure the confidence and co-operation of the staff involved; communication skills will be most important. In addition, the analyst must be able to grasp an overview of a particular area of work, at the same time as being able to deal with its intricate details.

Ways of sub-dividing the work of systems analysis are dealt with in Section 23.3.

23.2.3   The programmer

We saw in Unit 3 that the programmer is responsible for writing and testing programs according to specifications laid down by the systems analyst. In Unit 4 we saw that the programmer also assists the analyst during the stages of systems testing, implementation and maintenance. Clearly, in order to carry out these tasks effectively, the programmer must possess a logical mind and the ability to work at a very detailed level. Because of the high standard of documentation required at all stages of the work, and because of the need to adhere to stringent standards, a well-disciplined mind is needed. Section 23.3 deals with methods of sub-dividing programming work.

23.2.4   The operator

The operators are responsible for running the computer. They communicate with the machine via the console typewriter; they load stationery into the line printer; they mount tapes and disks onto their drive units; they ensure that jobs are correctly started, and that they end correctly, dealing with any exceptional conditions that arise.

In order to operate expensive and complex machinery thus, an operator must possess a sense of responsibility and an alert mind. The ability to work to rigid deadlines is also a prerequisite.

23.2.5   Data preparation

Data which is not in machine-sensible form has to be prepared for input to the computer, perhaps by being keyed onto magnetic disk; it is the data preparation personnel who carry out this task.

In an installation which uses magnetic disk as an input medium, operators key the data onto the disk from source documents, while verifier operators check their keying by repeating the process from the same documents. Similar tasks are carried out when other input media are in use, and in all cases data preparation instructions should be prepared to guide the data preparation staff.

23.2.6   Data control

Clearly, a link will be required between the department whose work is being carried out on the computer, and the computer room staff. The section responsible for ensuring that jobs flow smoothly through the computer room, and that work is carried out accurately, is known as the **data control section**. The data control clerks carry out the following tasks:

1   As and when laid down in the clerical procedures manual, the source documents containing the raw data which is to be input to a computer run are received from the relevant department. Control totals and counts will accompany this data (*see* Section 19.8).

2   The data will be visually checked and the totals and counts will be agreed. Any queries will have to be sorted out with the clerical staff who raised the data.

3   Batches of source documents will then be passed to the data preparation section, and a record kept of such batches. After keying and verification, the data, now in computer-sensible form, and the source documents, marked to show that they have been through the data preparation process, are passed back to the data control clerks.

4   Job assembly then takes place. Documents are drawn up showing the program(s), file(s) and output stationery needed for the run; the documents and the input are sent to the computer room. The job is then run.

5   When the output is received back in the control section, controls will be reconciled and queries dealt with. Having ensured that such ancillary operations as bursting and decollating have been carried out, the data control clerks send the output to the relevant user department.

23.2.7   The librarian

In a large organization, the computer department will be responsible for hundreds of operational programs and hundreds or thousands of files of crucial data. These programs and files will usually be held on magnetic tapes and disks. Clearly, a formal method of storing such a large volume of tape reels and disk packs will be required, and staff will be needed to supervise their use. The section of the computer department given these responsibilities is known as the library.

The librarian keeps records to allow the identification of the contents of each tape and each disk pack. Records are also kept each time a program or file is required by the computer operators. The librarian is responsible for the physical security of the magnetic media.

23.2.8   The database administrator

The role of the DBA was discussed in the previous chapter.

23.2.9   Running a typical batch job

The roles of the various staff discussed above can be better appreciated by examining how a typical batch processing job is handled in a large EDP department which uses a main-frame computer. The steps involved are:

1   The raw data is originated in the user department and collected together onto source documents. As appropriate, control totals and counts are prepared.

2   Periodically, as laid down in the user procedures manual, the source documents are sent to the data control section.

3   The data control clerks check the source data visually, and send it to the data preparation section. Here it may well be keyed onto magnetic disk.

4   When the data preparation task has been completed, the transaction file, along with the source documents, is returned to the data control section.

5   The data control section then request the librarian to send to them the current versions of the relevant programs and also the master file which was created during the last run of the system, which is now the brought-forward master file.

6   The programs and files are then sent to the operators, who run the job on the computer.

7   Intermediate results, such as the output from a validate program, will be sent back to the control section, and thence to the user department, for checking and correction as necessary.

8   When the whole job is completed, the programs and files are sent to the librarian for safekeeping, and the results are sent to the user department.

The process can be summarized as in Fig 23.1.

23.3   The structure of the department

23.3.1   The hierarchical approach

Having looked at the different functions which need to be carried out in a typical data processing department, we need to examine ways in which the staff carrying out those functions can be organized.

The structure adopted within a data preparation department will, clearly, depend upon several factors which will be unique to the particular organization concerned; among these factors will be the size of the department, the nature of the work, the history of

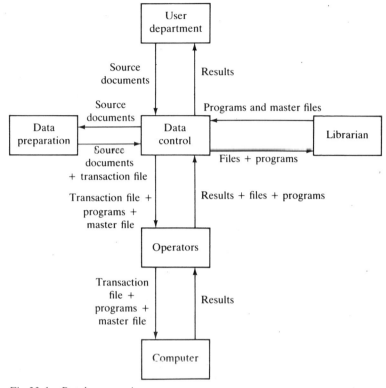

Fig 23.1   Batch processing

the data processing function, and the philosophy of the organiz-ation's management.

As will be expected, however, a 'traditional' approach to organ-izing effort within a DP department has grown up in the few years in which computers have been used. An organization chart depicting the structure of such a typical department is shown in Fig 23.2. The following points should be noted:

1   The department is divided into three major functions: analysis, programming and operations. Each function is headed by a manager who reports to the data processing manager.
2   A distinction is drawn on the chart in Fig 23.2 between applica-tion programmers, who write, test and maintain the application programs which the organization uses for carrying out its day-to-day processing tasks, and systems programmers, who modify or

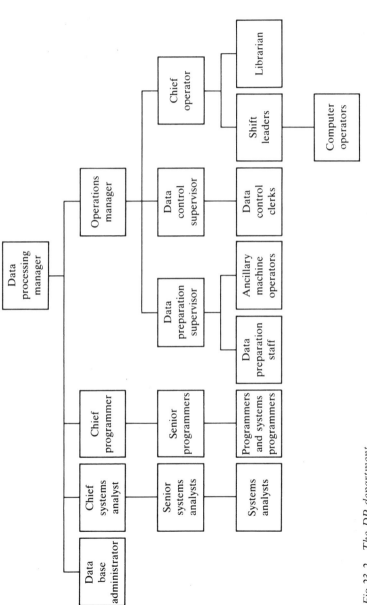

Fig 23.2   The DP department

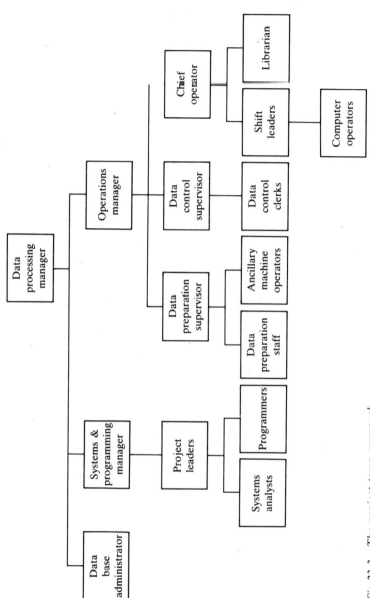

Fig 23.3   The project team approach

supplement the software provided by the computer manufacturer, so that the organization's individual needs can be met.

3 The operations manager is often made responsible for three separate sections: data preparation, data control and the computer room itself; each of these sections is headed by a supervisor.

4 In the chart in Fig 23.2, the ancillary machines are made the responsibility of the data preparation supervisor; many organizations place these machines under the supervisor of the operations section.

5 The librarian may report to the data control supervisor rather than to the operations supervisor.

23.3.2   The project team approach

An alternative to the traditional hierarchical approach outlined in the previous section is to organize programmers and analysts into project teams. This would result in an organization chart such as the one shown in Fig 23.3.

Using this approach, teams can be made permanently responsible for areas of work, such as personnel, accounts and others. The advantages which may be gained from the use of project teams include greater team spirit, better knowledge of a particular area of the organization's business and the benefits of specialization. Problems, however, may be encountered:

1 Work can be more difficult to schedule. Using the hierarchical approach, a task can easily be given to any available analyst or programmer; this is not so when staff are organized into project teams.

2 When the post of chief programmer is retained so that expert advice on programming matters can be given, conflicts of loyalty may arise. In such circumstances, a programmer may not know whether to respond to the project manager or to the chief programmer. Similar considerations could apply to analysts.

3 Much depends upon the quality of the team leaders.

A compromise approach is to use temporary teams for individual projects as and when they require staffing.

23.4   Problems and difficulties

Problems are encountered when staff are employed in any area of an organization, but the special staff problems found in computer work are worth considering here:

1   The technical nature of the work means that practitioners can rapidly become out-of-date. This means that time and effort have to be spent on keeping up-to-date, using appropriate training methods. This will be reflected in the costs and the timescales required for computer work.

2   The demanding nature of the work of the analyst and the programmer means that competent, experienced computer professionals are relatively scarce. In such a sellers' market, labour turnover is, inevitably, high. This means that high salaries have to be paid to computer personnel, and that they have to be given interesting work, in order that they will stay in one job for any length of time.

3   The problem outlined above is exacerbated by the fact that many computer personnel feel more loyal to the 'profession' of computing than they do to the organizations which employ them. This may lead to conflicts of interest and severe motivation problems among such staff, who may rebel against strict standards in such areas as documentation. In any case, whatever efforts a company makes to retain its staff, many will leave in order simply to gain wider experience of different hardware, languages and applications. This, they feel, furthers their long-term career prospects.

4   In a high-turnover situation, promotion will bring its problems, as few experienced people will be available internally to fill vacancies as they occur. The temptation to promote the best programmer to a vacant position in systems analysis, or the best analyst to a management role, must be resisted. Clearly, a careful analysis of the characteristics required by a person capable of filling the vacant job must first be made; it is little use promoting a member of staff to his/her level of incompetence.

5   The amount of maintenance work which has to be carried out in an installation can cause problems. Analysts and programmers prefer to work on development, which they see as more challenging and interesting, and as more useful to their career aspirations. Maintenance is often seen as uninteresting and routine work and yet, as time passes and more projects become operational, an increasingly high percentage of a computer department's time and effort will have to be spent on maintaining such live systems.

Some installations tackle the maintenance problem by making

analysts and programmers who are currently carrying out development work also responsible for maintaining live systems. This overcomes, to some extent, the boredom problem, because the personnel involved are dealing with a mixed workload. A second approach is to have a separate maintenance section, staffed by analysts and programmers who specialize in maintaining operational systems. After a new system has been developed and implemented, the manager of the maintenance section takes over responsibility for the system only if the system is sufficiently well-documented. This approach will probably lead to a better standard of documentation, and yet scheduling problems will be met; how are the maintenance personnel to be kept busy when little maintenance work is required?

Whatever approach towards maintenance is adopted, the ramifications in the area of labour turnover must be thought out.

23.5 The place of the department

The position of a data processing department within an organization depends upon many factors, among them the volume of work carried out by computer, the nature of the applications undertaken, the geographical spread of the organization's establishments, and the personalities and approach of the organization's management. Several general points, however, appear worthy of consideration.

Many years ago, when mechanized data processing systems came into widespread use, much of their work was carried out within the finance function. Because of this, many automatic data processing departments were made directly responsible to the chief accountant. With the advent of the computer, many organizations continued with this approach, but it soon became clear that several severe disadvantages ensued:

1 **Bias** is quite likely when job priorities are being set; functions other than the finance function may not have sufficient computing resources devoted to them.
2 A **restricted approach** to data processing, based on a limited accounting viewpoint, may be developed.
3 If a data processing manager is a member of the finance function, (s)he is not likely to carry sufficient **authority** when it comes to negotiations with potential users of the computer department's services, or with outside bodies.

A more common approach today is to make the EDP function a separate, independent department. Such a department can be guided by a steering committee, as suggested in Section 18.2, and it is often in a management services division, along with such specialisms as operational research and organization and methods. Such an approach has the following advantages:

1   The independent computing department can make its **services available equally** to all the major functions in the organization.
2   Independence encourages a **wide-ranging** view of the organization's data processing needs. Departmental boundaries do not necessarily impose artificial constraints on the work of the EDP personnel.
3   **Less conventional** solutions to problems can be tried.
4   Because the department has status and the full support of the top management, it will carry **authority**.
5   The location of all the management services functions in one department or division will be **mutually beneficial**.

23.6   Data processing standards in a main-frame environment

23.6.1   The need for standards

Many organizations are disappointed with the benefits gained from the introduction of computing facilities. One of the reasons for this is the fact that the working methods employed in many EDP departments are not of a sufficiently high quality; the use of standards is one answer to this problem.

23.6.2   The nature of standards

Standards are the internal rules by which computer personnel in a particular EDP department work; they embody the accepted best methods of carrying out all the activities which have to be performed in order that a computer installation can function.

A distinction is often made between methods standards and performance standards. **Methods standards** are guides to the way in which tasks in the computer department should be carried out; they lay down uniform practices and techniques. **Performance standards** act as yardsticks against which the performance of equipment and personnel can be measured and controlled.

23.6.3   The standards manual

An EDP department's standards should be documented in a standards manual. While the contents of such a document will vary from one installation to another, a typical manual will contain the following sections:

1   Administration and organization   This section introduces the manual. It outlines the structure of the EDP department, using an organization chart, and it describes the different jobs carried out therein. Any special rules relating to the work of the computer personnel are detailed.

2   The configuration   The computer hardware is described so that, inter alia, speeds and capacities are known.

3   Systems analysis   The methods of work relating to systems analysis are detailed, paying special attention to documentation standards and to control considerations.

4   Programming   The procedures relating to the writing, testing and maintenance of programs are specified.

5   Other tasks   The working methods of operators, data control clerks, librarians and data preparation staff are detailed.

6   Performance standards   Yardsticks against which the different types of personnel can be judged are laid down. Similar standards are specified for the computer hardware and other equipment.

23.6.4   The benefits gained

The advantages gained from the use of a carefully thought-out set of standards are as follows:

1   Computing facilities and computer personnel are expensive. If management is to reap the benefits of investing in such resources, an efficient approach to the solving of data processing problems should be laid down and adhered to.

2   The documenting of a common approach to work allows new staff to become useful members of the organization earlier.

3   Adherence to documentation standards allows for continuity. When staff leave, others can take over their work relatively easily. Similar considerations apply to hardware changes.

4   A good standards manual serves as a reference document for all data processing staff during the execution of their duties.

5   If standard procedures are laid down, planning, estimating and costing are more easily carried out.
6   Good standards facilitate control.

Of course, standards should always be viewed as a means to an end rather than an end in themselves. They should be changed over time to reflect changing circumstances, and they should be designed so that they do not stifle the initiative of staff or breed an inflexible approach; if they do either of these, staff will bypass or ignore them. Above all, the benefits gained from the use of standards should be worth while in terms of their cost.

23.7   End-user computing

The increased user-friendliness of computer software packages, along with the increased use of fourth-generation languages, has led to an increase in **end-user computing**, sometimes known as **end-user-driven computing**.

As non-specialists now have direct access to hands-on computing, the traditional role of the central DP department is changing, with less reliance on specialist analysts and programmers.

Some problems do arise with this change, though:

1   Duplication of work can easily arise, with one area of the organization unaware that a particular application or system has already been developed elsewhere.
2   Inconsistencies in the use of hardware and/or software can arise. This may mean that files or programs cannot readily be shared across the organization.
3   Non-specialists may give less attention to privacy and security than trained professionals.
4   As 'the wheel is being re-invented', mistakes are bound to be made by inexperienced and untrained staff.

One solution to these problems is the **information centre**. This is a small group of specialist computer staff, in an easily accessible location, who give advice to users on such matters as:

● the acquisition of hardware and software
● the technical aspects of using particular hardware or software
● access to data and programs in a distributed data processing

environment, perhaps where data needs to be downloaded from a central main-frame
- error detection and trouble-shooting
- the Data Protection Act
- the Computer Misuse Act

IC staff should be available on a 'drop-in' basis, and should have been equipped with all the software which the users may need to enquire about. Manuals and other literature must be available.

The IC should be responsible for running training courses, and it should be manned by staff who speak in plain English, rather than in 'Computerese'!

23.8 Summary

There are several ways of organizing a data processing department so that the best use is made of the expensive skills which are required. Data processing standards are used in an attempt to improve the work performance of data processing personnel.

Examination questions

I Draft the organization chart of a large computer department and outline the main duties of the sections reporting to the operations manager.

To whom do you think the data processing manager should be responsible? Give your reasons.

(Chartered Association of Certified Accountants)

2 ABC Ltd's computer department contains some 35 members of staff, including the computer manager. Analysts and programmers work together in project teams under team leaders.

Required:

(a) Draft what in your opinion would be a typical organization chart for this computer department. The distribution of staff should be clearly shown.

(b) Identify the principal responsibilities of the operations manager in a computer department.

(Chartered Association of Certified Accountants)

3 (a) Draft the organization chart of a computer department of 40 staff. Your chart should show clearly how the staff are distributed in the department and any assumptions made must be stated.

(b)   Give a concise outline of the principal duties of a systems analyst during the life of a systems project.

(Chartered Association of Certified Accountants)

4   Your company is considering the installation of a medium-sized batch processing computer. You are required to outline:

(a)   the organization to be set up to manage the proposed facility, showing:

● the main sections; and

● the types of staff required in each section;

(b)   the principal duties of the data processing manager and of any two of the sectional managers.

(Institute of Cost and Management Accountants)

5   Give a description of the duties for one of the following data processing personnel:

(a)   data processing manager

(b)   computer operator

(c)   data preparation supervisor

(d)   systems analyst

(e)   programmer

6   At 9.30 a.m. on Tuesday in a normal working week, the wages section of XYZ Ltd sends its transaction and amendment data to the computer department. At 4.00 p.m. (1600 hrs) on Wednesday, the wages section receives paylists, payslips and other printed results back from the computer department.

Give a detailed account of the activities which would typically take place in the computer department between the receipt of the payroll data and the despatch of results back to the wages section.

(Chartered Association of Certified Accountants)

7   In a well-administered computer department there usually exists a data processing standards manual.

(a)   Outline the format and content of a typical standards manual, explaining the sources of the material within it.

(b)   Explain what purposes are served by data processing standards.

(Chartered Association of Certified Accountants)

8   A centralized payroll and labour costing system is used by many subsidiaries of a large organization. All the master data needed to calculate standard payments are held on disk files at the computer centre. Variations, where appropriate, are supplied by the pay section in each subsidiary on specially designed forms, and data preparation is carried out centrally on a key-to-disk system.

Required:

(a) Describe the techniques, both manual and computer, which may be used to ensure that only correct data are processed in the payroll system.

(b) What are the responsibilities of the data control section in such a system?

(Chartered Association of Certified Accountants)

9 What are the benefits of end-user computing? What problems does it pose? How can these problems be overcome?

24

The data processing industry

24.1 Introduction

Having gained an understanding of the considerations which need to be taken into account when a computer installation is being staffed, we next examine some of the organizations which make up 'the computer industry'.

24.2 Computer manufacturers

Computer manufacturers supply hardware and software to organizations who wish to use computing facilities. Direct sale or rental is often used, and it is also quite common for manufacturers to sell hardware and software to leasing companies, who then lease it to the users.

International Business Machines (IBM) dominates the world computer market. Other companies of note are Digital, NEC, Fujitsu, Unisys, Hitachi, Wang, NCR and Hewlett Packard.

Many small organizations also exist which supply peripheral equipment which is compatible with the hardware provided by the large manufacturers; some of them also supply memory.

24.3 The bureau

24.3.1 The nature of the bureau

A bureau is an organization which provides its clients with computer-related services. Bureaux are thus also known as service bureaux or data processing service centres.

Computer bureaux carry out a wide range of tasks, on either a continuous or an ad hoc basis; some of these tasks are:

1 A full service which entails the bureau's staff carrying out all the stages of computerization for a client.
2 Systems analysis and design.
3 Program writing and testing.
4 A 'do it yourself' service which allows the user's own staff to run the programs on the bureau's machine.
5 Hiring out computer time and computer operators, so that clients can run programs.
6 Timesharing, which allows users to access the bureau's powerful central machine from their own premises using terminals and a communication link.
7 Data preparation; a bureau may specialize in, say, OCR documents, as well as providing the normal service of converting source documents into machine-sensible media such as magnetic disks.
8 Software provision; a bureau may sell or lease application packages or subroutines.
9 Advice and consultancy; this can range from assistance with decisions about hardware acquisition to advice concerning the implementation of a system, or the training of personnel. Whenever consultants are employed, however, it is always wise to remember the word's first syllable!

Clearly, not every bureau offers all of the above services; many bureaux specialize in terms of the tasks which they carry out, the industry they serve, or the type of application with which they deal.

24.3.2 Types of bureaux

A computer bureau is often an independent body set up specifically to provide one or more of the services listed above. Computer manufacturers also set up service centres. Where a computer user with spare capacity offers it for sale to others, then the user is acting, in effect, as a bureau.

24.3.3 Reasons for using a bureau

An organization uses the services of a computer bureau for one or more of the following reasons:

1 Where an organization cannot afford to buy, rent, or lease a large computer or where it feels that the money required to do so could be better spent elsewhere.

2 Where the acquisition of an 'in-house' main-frame computer would not be cost-effective because the workload is insufficient to justify it.

3 Where the workload peaks, perhaps at year-end or the end of a quarter, and the existing systems, manual or computerized, cannot cope with the extra volume of transactions.

4 Where one-off jobs have to be tackled. An example could be a large volume of data preparation required when converting a manual file to magnetic disk during a system's implementation.

5 When standby facilities are required in case the organization's own computer fails.

6 When specialist knowledge about a particular aspect of electronic data processing is not present within the organization.

7 If a company is considering the acquisition of a computer or a piece of hardware, it can gain experience of the equipment at a bureau before making a final decision; this consideration also applies to software.

8 Once the decision to acquire a computer has been taken, the organization can use a bureau's facilities to develop and test the systems which it wishes to run initially on the machine.

9 The organization may not wish to take on the responsibility of running its own computer department, preferring instead to rely on the specialists employed by bureaux. A company may believe that, by so doing, it can gain access to up-to-date hardware, software and expertise, and that the bureau's costs are thereby shared among many users.

24.3.4   The problems and difficulties

When considering using the services of a bureau, an organization should carefully consider the following points:

1 When data processing is undertaken outside the organization, then control over that processing must be lost to some extent. The bureau's reputation and standing must, therefore, be above question.

2 Because a bureau will have many clients, all wanting the results of their data processing immediately (or sooner!), an individual organization may have to wait for information which is required there and then. Where turnaround time is an important consideration, a bureau may thus not be the best solution.

3   A bureau's staff will not be so committed to a user's needs as his/her own staff would be; this may, in certain circumstances, lead to work of a lower standard.

4   When a system is developed and written by a bureau, there will be a lack of continuity once the system has been implemented. Because of this, strict adherence to standards, particularly in the area of documentation, must be insisted upon during the development stage.

5   Control over accuracy will be more of a problem when processing is undertaken at a point which is physically remote from the user's premises. While these problems can be overcome, extra costs will be involved.

6   Security of sensitive information will not be easy when an outside body is carrying out an organization's data processing.

7   The cost of a bureau's services must, of course, be carefully considered.

24.4   Software houses

The term 'software house' covers a wide variety of organizations, ranging from large companies which offer analysis and programming services, off-the-shelf application packages or tailor-made systems to individuals or small partnerships which write programs on an ad-hoc basis. In all cases, the standing of such an organization must be thoroughly investigated before its services are made use of.

Examples of software houses which market microcomputer software are Ashton Tate (dBASE IV), Lotus (Lotus 1-2-3) and Microsoft (MS Works and MS DOS). Software companies like Microsoft utilize 'usability labs' where software can be tested on people with various levels of computer experience prior to design decisions actually being made.

24.5   Leasing companies

An alternative to buying or renting equipment directly from a computer manufacturer is to use the services of a leasing company. A leasing company buys hardware from a manufacturer and then leases it to the user, typically on a five or seven year contract. The pros and cons of such an approach are dealt with in Chapter 25. Many banks have leasing subsidiaries, and finance houses and merchant banks also offer the service. Equipment brokers deal with second-hand equipment.

24.6 Other organizations

The British Computer Society is a professional society for personnel involved in computing. Admission to membership is by examination.

The National Computing Centre, sponsored by the government, publishes books, runs training courses, and provides advice and other services.

Examination questions

1 Write notes on the services provided by:
   (a) software houses
   (b) computer manufacturers
   (c) bureaux
2 (a) Describe the range of services offered by computer bureaux.

   (b) List the major features which should be considered when choosing a computer bureau.

   (Chartered Association of Certified Accountants)

Unit Six

The implications of computer use

25

Acquiring a computer

25.1 Introduction

We now have an understanding of the way in which computer systems are designed and developed, and we have examined the job functions within, and the structure of, the typical computer installation. In this unit we attempt to answer three very important questions:

1 How does an organization decide whether or not to acquire computing facilities and, if it decides that computing facilities are needed, how does it go about procuring them cost-effectively?
2 Once computing facilities have been acquired, how does the organization ensure that processing is carried out accurately?
3 What are the legal implications of computer use?

25.2 The benefits of computerization

We begin our examination of the way in which decisions concerning the acquisition of computing facilities are made by looking at the reasons which may prompt an organization to consider computerization in the first place.

The benefits which may be gained from the use of a computer

are:

1 The computer is **fast**. We saw in Unit 2 that the speed of a large computer's central processing unit is measured in MIPS, or millions of instructions per second; we also saw that even a slow peripheral like the line printer outputs information at the rate of 2000 or so characters per second. Despite the fact that human beings have to prepare data for input to the computer and distribute the resulting information, these speeds mean that information for management can be produced sooner, so that improved decision-making can result.

2 Because of this high speed, a **better service** may well be given to customers, who find that enquiries are answered more quickly, orders are despatched more promptly and parts are out-of-stock less frequently.

3 The high speeds at which computers work also mean that better **information** can be produced. Huge amounts of data can be sifted through and summarized in short periods of time, and the management by exception approach, which relies on managers being directed to those areas requiring their attention, can be employed.

4 The speed of the computer allows it to tackle jobs which would **not be physically possible without it**. Operational research applications, which perhaps involve hundreds of millions of calculations, are an example.

5 As the machine's speed allows it to deal with a **huge volume** of transactions, it can allow savings to be made in the costs of staff, equipment and space; huge files of data can be held on magnetic tapes or disks.

6 The computer is **versatile**. As we saw in Unit 2, the machine can carry out any task, provided that we can tell it how to perform that task. Once such a general-purpose machine has been acquired, then, it can be used in any area of the business.

7 Because of their speed of operation, computers can be considered **flexible**, in that they can deal more easily than can manual systems with the increased workloads which occur when activity peaks. For example, a computer system, once implemented, can deal easily with 10 000 transactions or 100 000, provided that the input can be made available and the output dealt with.

8 The computer is **diligent** and **reliable**; it will not absent itself from work due to sickness, and it will not arrive late or spend long lunch hours over a beer! Once a program has begun execution, operation is **automatic**, and no further human intervention is needed; this means that the millionth calculation in a job will be carried out just as accurately as was the first.

9 Computer processing, once programs and systems have been thoroughly tested, will be completely **accurate**. Hardware malfunctions are extremely rare, and are usually detected by the self-checking routines which are built into the machine when it is manufactured.

10 As we saw in Unit 4, a thorough **investigation** and **analysis** of a business operation needs to be carried out before that operation can be computerized. In the course of everyday work, such an analysis is not usually undertaken – there is no time. The introduction of a main-frame computer into an organization often affords the opportunity for such studies to be carried out, and even areas of business which are not directly affected by the machine can benefit from this.

11 All of the above points mean that, in the right circumstances, the use of a computer will be **cost-effective**, calculations requiring the work of an employee for a year being carried out for a few pence. This is shown on the graph in Fig 25.1, where, for the sake of simplicity, the average costs of manual data processing are assumed to be constant regardless of the volume of transactions dealt with.

Note the break-even point; below this volume of transactions it is not worth using a computer. It should further be noted that, as manual costs constantly rise due to wage increases, the costs of

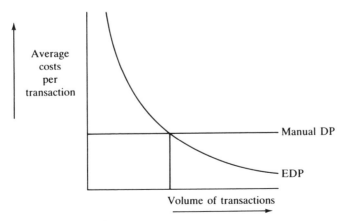

Fig 25.1 Processing costs

computerized processing are rapidly falling. More and more companies can thus use computers for more and more tasks: this is the 'widening and deepening' of computer use.

25.3   The problems and difficulties

The use of a computer for the carrying out of commercial data processing work carries with it, however, several disadvantages:

1   Computers are costly. If a large machine is purchased, then the initial costs are high; if rental or leasing is opted for, then a substantial periodic outlay is required. In all cases, staff costs will have to be met. If follows from these considerations that an organization should think very carefully before it commits itself to acquiring computing facilities.

2   The **technology** of computing is moving very fast. A user runs the risk of losing money because the hardware and/or software used has become obsolete.

3   The introduction of computerized data processing systems usually causes **disruption**. This is because methods of work will have to be altered to fit in with the computer systems, and because structural changes within the organization will sometimes be necessary. These problems are exacerbated by the fact that computer systems are not developed and implemented overnight; it will be several years before all the work which is going to be computerized has been taken on. During this transition period, there will be problems.

4   The **human problems** related to this disruption must never be overlooked. Staff will be fearful concerning the future, perhaps believing that their jobs may be reduced to repetitive exercises in form filling, and that they will be expected to work to near-impossible deadlines; they may be concerned about status, feeling that their decision-making responsibilities will be taken away from them; they may be worried about redundancy. All of these factors will affect morale, and may have repercussions in terms of an organization's rate of labour turnover. In all cases, management will have to re-think carefully its policies on such matters as recruitment, training, promotion and career development.

5   The computer is often accused of **de-humanizing** relationships, perhaps those between an organization and its employees, or between an organization and its customers. Where such an accusation can fairly be levelled at a computerized system then, clearly,

something is amiss, and a thorough re-appraisal of that system is called for.

6   Once a company invests heavily in computing, and carries out much of its data processing this way, it is **vulnerable** to a failure in either the hardware, the software, or the personnel upon which it has come to rely. When a computerized system fails, it will not be possible to revert to the old manual system, as this will have been discontinued, and its staff and equipment redeployed. Organizations often make reciprocal standby arrangements with other users of similar computing facilities, so that such eventualities can be met, but these cost money and they are not always satisfactory.

7   However careful the work of the analysts and programmers who designed and developed a particular system, there is always the possibility of error in computerized data processing procedures. As we saw in Unit 4, it is impossible to test thoroughly a system so that its complete accuracy under all circumstances can be guaranteed. Furthermore, when errors creep into the processing carried out by a computer system, they may be difficult to detect and difficult to purge from master files.

8   **Master file information** held within a computerized system is always susceptible to loss through errors made by that system or by the staff running it. Precautions taken in this area will include the keeping of duplicate copies of master files at remote locations, but, once again, this will add to costs.

9   Because records within an EDP system are **not visible** in the usual way, it will be more difficult to check that errors are not happening. The job of the auditor, discussed in Chapter 26, will be more difficult.

10   Computer systems are susceptible to **fraud** by knowledgeable persons, and the design of any system should take careful account of this.

11   If a data processing task is being carried out manually, then minor changes to the system of work can be handled quickly and cheaply; all that is required is a memorandum to the clerks concerned which outlines the new procedures. Even more complex changes can be handled relatively easily. But once a former clerical task has been taken over by the computer and the new system has been developed, tested and implemented, that system becomes relatively **inflexible**. Even minor changes need to be specified, programmed and tested, and the new version of the system has to be documented and implemented. Of course, the ease with which a system can be changed will depend, in part, upon the quality of the

original systems design, but it will not always be possible, or desirable, to build much flexibility into a new system. In all cases, the user's needs will have to be carefully ascertained before the system is designed, so that future, costly, changes are less likely to be required.

12　A final point concerning the problems of computer use is that, contrary to what many people in an organization may believe, the machine is **not a universal panacea** for all ills. Only certain problems can be tackled cost-effectively on the machine, and the method of solving those problems, as the reader is by now only too aware, will have to be clearly and completely defined beforehand. This should always be borne in mind.

25.4　Other effects of the computer

Other implications, not so easily classified as benefits or disadvantages, will follow from the introduction of a computer:

1　A change will take place at the middle and lower management levels in terms of decision-making. Many routine decisions and tasks, formerly the responsibility of staff in this area, will now be taken over by the computer. This may result in fewer such managers being employed, but it will also have the effect of freeing those who remain from the more mundane tasks, thereby allowing them to concentrate on more crucial decisions. The more widespread use of expert systems will hasten this 'de-layering' in many organizations.

2　If routine clerical tasks, in such areas as invoicing and payroll, are to be carried out by the computer, then there will inevitably be a consequent change in organization structure. Departments or sections which formerly carried out such tasks will perhaps be reduced in size, combined with others, or even abolished altogether. Where systems are developed which are inter-departmental in nature, for example integrated systems using the database approach, these ramifications can be even more wide-reaching.

3　The introduction of large-scale computing into an organization will have profound effects on the role of that organization's management. As we have seen, the computer will provide better information for decision makers at all levels but, as we have also noted, those who use the computer will have to carefully specify their information needs well in advance, so that the appropriate systems can be developed and implemented. Computerized information processing thus demands a team of managers who are able to identify those areas of their business to which the computer can make a cost-effective contribution and, just as important, those areas where it is not appropriate to employ the machine.

4   The use of a computer will, inevitably, add to the number of specialists employed by an organization. Where tensions already exist between 'line' and 'staff' personnel, these may well be exacerbated.

5   The amount of decentralization practised in an organization may well be affected by the introduction of a computer, although the nature of the change depends on the particular circumstances found in that organization. Clearly, if a large data bank is located at the headquarters, decision-making can be centralized, and local units may find their initiative stifled. Where a system is employed which allows staff at branches to have access to information on a real-time basis, however, the reverse effect may be the result.

In all cases, the effects discussed in the last three sections should be carefully considered before any large-scale computerization is undertaken; the introduction of a computer, after all, will have wide-reaching effects for the organization and those employed by it.

25.5   The costs of main-frame computer use

We have seen that one of the problems encountered when a computer is used for data processing tasks is the resulting costs, both once-off costs and recurring costs. The initial costs which will have to be met are:

1   The cost of the study which is carried out in order to determine whether computing facilities are required and how those facilities should be provided. The **feasibility study** is dealt with fully in Section 25.7.

2   The cost of the accommodation which will house the computer and the personnel employed within the data processing department. Whether new accommodation is to be built, or existing premises are to be converted, these costs will be considerable. Expensive air-conditioning equipment will be required in the computer room.

3   Equipment costs; under this heading must be included;
●   the cost of the hardware itself
●   the cost of the data preparation equipment, the ancillary

machines such as bursters and decollators, and the storage facilities required to hold disks, stationery and other media
● the cost of furniture and office equipment.
4   The one-off cost of installing the equipment.
5   File media, input media and stationery costs.
6   Before useful work can be commenced on the machine, soft ware costs will have to be incurred. Depending on the nature of the installation's requirements, this may include an operating system, service programs and application packages.
7   The costs of recruiting and training the personnel who will initially staff the EDP department.
8   The development and implementation costs of the systems which will be initially run on the new machine.

The recurring costs of running a computer department on an operational basis are:

1   The cost of accommodation, in terms of rent, rates and services.
2   The cost of the equipment, which is often rented or leased; a maintenance contract covering the computer hardware will have to be negotiated, and standby arrangements which protect the user against the hardware being 'off-the-air' will need to be made.
3   The cost of enhancing existing software, or of acquiring new software.
4   Staff costs; these include the costs of recruiting and training new staff, and staff wages and salaries. The rate of labour turnover will affect the amount of expenditure required in this area.
5   The ongoing costs such as power and stationery.
6   The costs of administering the computer department.
7   Insurance of equipment and premises.

When attempting to evaluate the costs of computer usage, the following methods can be used:

1   The **payback method,** which tries to establish the time it will take for the savings made to match the expenditure incurred. This somewhat crude method does not take account of the timings of costs and benefits, but is relatively easy to calculate.
2   **Discounted cash flow methods,** such as net present value (NPV) and internal rate of return (IRR), try to take account of the timing of inflows and outflows of cash. By discounting future money, such

systems recognize the fact that money coming in today is worth more than money which will be received in a year's time, and so a more realistic estimate of the value of an investment can be made.

25.6 Methods of financing the costs

25.6.1 Introduction

There are several ways of acquiring computing facilities and financing the consequent costs. The four commonest methods used are purchase, rental, leasing and using the services of a bureau. Each of these is discussed in what follows but, throughout, the reader should bear in mind that each set of circumstances, and each contract signed, will require careful and detailed consideration.

25.6.2 Purchasing a computer

Computers can be purchased from computer manufacturers. The advantages of this approach are:

1 Where it is envisaged that a machine will be used for a long period, perhaps five or more years, outright purchase may be cheaper than any other method.
2 As outright purchase gives the user ownership of the machine, (s)he can use it as (s)he pleases; there will be no extra charges levied as a result of the amount of work carried out by the computer, as there often are when a machine is rented.
3 Once a machine has been bought, there are no regular outlays as there are when a computer is rented.
4 There may be tax advantages.
5 Manufacturers are prepared to agree maintenance contracts for hardware purchased in this way.
6 As the computer is an asset of the organization which has purchased it, that organization can dispose of it for cash as required, although the value of a second-hand machine will depend very much on whether or not it has become obsolete over time.

The disadvantages of outright purchase are:

1 As computers cost a lot of money, an organization's cash flow may well be seriously affected by the one-off cost of purchasing a machine. Even where a company can afford to buy a computer, it is possible that the money could be better spent elsewhere in order to achieve a higher return.

2   When an organization purchases a computer, it must use that machine for several years in order to recoup its investment. But if computer technology is developing fast, a machine may become obsolete after a few years. In such a case, a loss may be suffered if a computer has to be sold earlier than was anticipated.

3   When a company purchases a computer, it acquires a machine of the appropriate size and power for the work which is going to be done. Even in a short period of time, however, this workload can alter dramatically and the computer can prove too small (or too large!) for the tasks which it is employed to carry out. Clearly, the purchaser of a computer loses the flexibility of being allowed to cope easily with such circumstances.

25.6.3   Renting a computer

Potential computer users may acquire hardware for use at their own premises by renting it from a computer manufacturer. When this is done, a fixed monthly charge is levied, and extra charges, which depend upon the amount of work carried out by the machine, are often written into the contract, too. The monthly charge for renting computer equipment thus is often one forty-eighth of its purchase price. The advantages of renting a computer are:

1   No large one-off payment is required; this helps the liquidity position of the organization concerned, and allows the cash thus retained to be used elsewhere in the business.

2   The rental method allows an organization to plan its cashflow more easily.

3   A rental agreement will cover a fixed period of time. This gives the computer-user more flexibility, as an unwanted machine can be disposed of at the end of the agreed rental period without loss; rental is thus an attractive proposition in time of great technological change.

4   As maintenance is usually included in a rental agreement, the user has some measure of protection against the failure of the hardware. Some rental agreements stipulate that charges will only be levied if a specified number of trouble-free computing hours are achieved in a period.

5   Once a rental contract has been signed, inflation cannot affect the charges agreed.

6 There may be tax advantages.

The disadvantages of the rental method are:

1 A fixed monthly outlay has to be met throughout the period of computer use. Over a long period, perhaps five years or more, this will usually prove a more expensive way of financing computing facilities than purchase.
2 The computer remains the property of the manufacturer, and never becomes an asset of the company concerned.
3 The monthly outlay increases when extra charges are levied for extra work done.
4 Rental charges do not reduce after a specified period, as leasing charges often do.

25.6.4 Leasing a computer

We saw in Chapter 24 that an alternative to purchasing or renting computer equipment is the use of the services of a leasing company. In such circumstances, the leasing company buys the hardware and, after it has been installed on the user's premises, the user begins to pay monthly leasing charges to the lessor. In many respects, then, computer leasing arrangements are very similar to those employed when any equipment is being leased.

Leasing contracts are often for longer periods than rental agreements, and lower charges are usually made. If a lease is renewed, even lower charges are often agreed. The advantages of leasing computer equipment are:

1 The advantages of renting computer equipment, which were discussed above, will apply, to some extent, to leasing.
2 Further advantages accrue because leasing charges are usually lower than those for rental, because a renewal of a lease is usually agreed at a lower rate still, and because no extra charges are made for extra work undertaken.
3 Leasing contracts can be tailor-made to suit an individual organization's requirements, even to the extent of matching the cash-flow profile of the equipment.

The disadvantages of leasing are:

1 Similar disadvantages to the first two noted above under rental apply still. In addition, the period involved in a leasing contract is usually longer than that covered by a rental contract, and so the user loses some of the flexibility given by renting.

2 Leasing companies will only purchase and lease the equipment of certain well-known manufacturers; this is so that they can be reasonably sure of re-leasing equipment after it has been returned to them. It means, however, that a computer user wishing to lease equipment has less choice.

3 Manufacturers may refuse to agree maintenance contracts for equipment which is leased after a certain period of time. This may cause difficulties for the users, and so it must be clarified before a leasing contract is signed.

25.6.5   Using a bureau

We saw in Chapter 24 that an alternative to the acquisition of 'in-house' computing equipment is the use of the services offered by a bureau. The advantages and disadvantages of such an approach are discussed in Sections 24.3.3 and 24.3.4.

25.7   The computer feasibility study

25.7.1   The need for a feasibility study

We have examined, in this chapter, the effects of the introduction of main-frame computing facilities into an organization, and the methods of financing the costs involved; it will now be clear that the acquisition of computing facilities is a major step for any organization to take. In this section we discuss how decisions in this area are taken.

A computer feasibility study is carried out in order to determine:

1 whether or not a case exists for the introduction of computing facilities into an organization;
2 if such a case is found to exist, what type of equipment, in terms of its make, capacity and other characteristics, should be acquired;
3 how such equipment should be financed; should it be purchased, rented or leased, or should the services of a bureau be opted for;
4 what the timescale for the installation of the required equipment, and the implementation of those systems which are to be initially run on it, will be;

5 the wider implications of the introduction of electronic data processing into the organization.

A careful distinction should be drawn between the project feasibility study and the computer feasibility study. As we saw in Chapter 18, the project feasibility study is carried out to determine whether or not a particular project should be computerized, once a computer has been acquired.

25.7.2 The steering committee

Before any work concerning the possible acquisition of computing facilities is undertaken, a steering committee should be formed. We saw in Chapter 18 that such a committee guides the work of the computer department once it has been set up and become operational. Another of its functions is to supervise the team carrying out the initial computer feasibility study, and to lend its support to the team, which should report frequently to the steering committee.

The steering committee should consist of a number of high-level personnel from all areas of the company's operations. Of course, some computer knowledge is called for.

25.7.3 The preliminary study

Before a full feasibility study is undertaken, a preliminary study should be carried out. The preliminary study consists of an examination of the work likely to be undertaken by a computer, and the likely costs and benefits. It will thus enable management to determine whether the full feasibility study will be worth while, and it will allow objectives to be set for the full feasibility study. If it becomes clear during the preliminary study that a computer would not be the answer to the organization's problems, then no further work need be undertaken.

25.7.4 The feasibility study

Once the objectives of the feasibility study have been determined, the study can take place. A detailed investigation of all areas of the organization's business will be carried out and a schedule will be drawn up of all current and future applications which could be tackled by means of electronic data processing. Careful estimates of the volume of work, the likely increase in workload, and the current costs of processing, will have to be made, and special attention will need to be paid to such matters as time factors, deadlines and unusual processing requirements.

Clearly, members of the organization's own staff will act as members of the study team, as they will have a sound knowledge of the structure and operation of the business. Personnel from outside bodies may also take part in the study, so that specialized knowledge of computers and the ways in which they can be used can be brought in.

25.7.5   Asking for quotations

Once a schedule has been drawn up which details the work that will be carried out by means of the envisaged computing facilities, the major manufacturers and bureaux, if such an approach is deemed appropriate, can be approached and asked to quote. Based upon the work detailed in the schedule, a manufacturer should be able to specify:

1   the hardware and software which would allow the potential user to carry out the required tasks;

2   the costs of purchasing, renting or, where appropriate, leasing such hardware and software;

3   the maintenance support offered by the manufacturer for the proposed hardware and software, and the cost of such support;

4   the standby facilities provided by the manufacturer in case of equipment failure, and the cost of providing the service. The manufacturer should at least be able to provide a list of other users of similar equipment who could be approached with a view to the making of a reciprocal standby arrangement;

5   training supplied by the manufacturer, and its cost;

6   other advice and support provided;

7   delivery dates of the suggested systems; installation details;

8   the special facilities needed by the hardware, and the cost of these;

9   the suitability of the proposed system for handling possible increases in the organization's volume of work; can peripheral units be easily added; is the machine capable of being replaced by a larger one in the manufacturer's range without extensive re-programming – is, in other words, 'upward compatibility' built into the system?

25.7.6 The decision

When the replies have been received from the organizations which were asked to tender, they should be carefully evaluated. The most promising replies can be followed up and further investigations can be made. Test runs of programs which are thought to be typical of those which will run when the organization's systems become operational can be carried out to compare the performance of different hardware and software; such **benchmark tests** attempt to test different machines under the same conditions but, of course, severe problems are encountered when such comparisons are being made.

When a thorough evaluation of the alternatives proposed has been made, a decision can be taken. Bearing in mind the cost implications of all possible courses of action, the team will propose that: no action be taken; **or** a particular model of machine should be bought, or rented, or leased; **or** the services of a bureau should be used. The decisions taken will be documented in the feasibility report.

25.7.7 The feasibility report

The computer feasibility report should contain the following sections:

1 an introduction which gives the background to the study;
2 the recommendations; the chosen hardware should be specified, and the necessary software should be detailed;
3 a method of acquiring the selected hardware and software should be recommended;
4 a justification of the decision should be made in financial terms. The hardware and software opted for should be costed, as should the alternative solutions which have been rejected;
5 the timetable for the installation of the new system;
6 changes which are likely to be required over time, in view of the likely growth in the volume of the organization's work, should be specified;
7 the wider implications of computerization, for example the effects on staff.

Once the feasibility report has been agreed by the steering committee, it can be forwarded to the board of directors for a decision.

25.8   Acquiring a microcomputer

Clearly, when a microcomputer is being acquired, then all the stages which are outlined in the previous section would seem a little like overkill!

It is important, however, that a correct decision is made, and the user must carry out a study of his/her needs, including the applications to be carried out on the machine, and the sizes of the various files intended, both now and in the future. The sort of after-sales service provided by the organization selling the package is also a critical factor.

25.9   Summary

Today, a great variety of computer hardware and software is available to the potential user of computing facilities. Because of this, and because the introduction of electronic data processing will have far-reaching effects on an organization, a feasibility study should be carried out before any decisions concerning the acquisition of computing facilities are made.

Examination questions

1 (a)   Tabulate, under main headings, the principal types of expenditure to which you consider the costs of running a computer department should be allocated.

(b)   What benefits might an organization gain from a newly-installed computer installation?

(Chartered Association of Certified Accountants)

2   An 'in-house' computer can be acquired by rental, leasing or purchase. What financial factors have to be considered when making the choice of method?

List the advantages and disadvantages of purchasing a computer.

3   What are the advantages and disadvantages of leasing a computer?

4   What are the advantages and disadvantages of using a computer bureau?

5 (a)   Describe briefly the type of service which the computer bureau industry provides for its customers.

(b)   Give five advantages for using a bureau for data processing.

6 Assume that your company's hourly payroll is prepared by a bureau. List with a brief explanation:

(a) three examples of transaction or amendment data which would need to be despatched to the bureau weekly;

(b) three examples of information which would be received back from the bureau.

(Chartered Association of Certified Accountants)

7 Describe the advantages and disadvantages of the use of a computer bureau to process data, as compared with the use of a company's own computer installation.

(Institute of Chartered Accountants)

8 Assume that you are the accountant of a small company, XYZ Ltd. You are considering having the company's payroll prepared by a local computer bureau. What are the major points on which you would seek information during your discussions with the manager of the bureau?

(Chartered Association of Certified Accountants)

9 (a) What is a computer feasibility study?

(b) Why is such a study a prerequisite to the introduction of a computer into a business organization?

10 Why is a computer feasibility study necessary? Describe the cost information that you would expect to find in a feasibility report.

11 The directors of a company consider that it may be advantageous to install a computer and you have been asked to advise on the stages that would be involved from this point until the computer became fully operational.

You are required to list these stages and give brief details of each.

(Institute of Chartered Accountants).

12 Your company has invited proposals from computer manufacturers for a computer configuration which is to be installed.

Under the following headings briefly describe or list the type of information that should be included:

(a) equipment   (e) standby
(b) delivery   (f) installation requirements
(c) maintenance   (g) software
(d) training   (h) other facilities and charges

13 A feasibility study is the investigation an organization undertakes of its various activities to establish whether or not the use of electronic data processing equipment can be justified.

Required:

(a) list the factors which may prompt a firm to institute such a survey and

(b)   outline the stages of a typical study in a medium-sized organization.

(Chartered Association of Certified Accountants)

14   Draw up a checklist of the information you would seek from a computer manufacturer prior to making a decision to purchase computer equipment. You are to assume that you are seeking to acquire a medium to large installation.

(Chartered Association of Certified Accountants)

26
Control and audit considerations

26.1   Introduction

In Units 2 to 4 of this book, we discussed computer hardware, programming, and systems analysis and design. Throughout those units, we repeatedly came across the fact that there is always a chance of errors creeping into a data processing system, unless the user of that system takes specific steps to eliminate those errors. In the course of the text, as we came across situations in which we thought there was a possibility of errors occurring, we outlined the precautions that computer people take in an attempt to eliminate that possibility. In this chapter we attempt to pull together all the loose strands concerning the control of data processing activities which we have come across to date.

We look first at the different types of errors that the management of a computer installation should be on their guard against and then, in the light of those errors, we consider how the computer affects the role and function of the auditor.

26.2   Types of error

There are many ways of classifying the different types of error that can occur when data is processed electronically and each classification is somewhat arbitrary. For our purposes, we shall consider the following six sources of inaccuracy, and ways in which computer personnel attempt to eliminate them:

- hardware errors
- software errors
- faulty systems design
- faulty programming
- mistakes by the operator
- errors in the input

In addition, we shall briefly consider fraud and physical security.

26.3   Hardware errors

Hardware errors are very rare nowadays, as computers have built-in self-checking circuitry. Some of the checks that we came across in Unit 2, when we discussed hardware, were:

- parity checks
- check-reading, for example where the data from an input medium is read twice to ensure accuracy
- read after write checks; data which has been written to magnetic tape is read back and compared with what should have been written
- echo checks in data transmission systems
- the checking of magnetic media trailer labels to ensure that no blocks have been lost from a tape file

26.4   Software errors

Errors in the software supplied by third parties will not often be the cause of errors in a data processing installation, but new software, or early use of an updated version of an existing piece of software, may cause problems. Thus, when no other possible source of error seems to be the cause of a particular problem, it may be worth suspecting a compiler, an operating system or an application package, but this should normally only be done as a last resort.

Clearly, one way to avoid software errors is only to use the tried and tested products of reputable organizations, but if everybody followed this advice, nothing new would ever be written! In all cases, thorough testing and/or parallel running of new systems under actual operating conditions should be undertaken in an attempt to identify, inter alia, such software problems.

26.5 Faulty systems analysis

As we saw in Unit 4, many tasks have to be carried out during the investigation, design, development and implementation of a new system. If any of those tasks are not carried out sufficiently thoroughly, then the resulting system may not produce the desired results accurately. Several solutions to problems in this area can be suggested:

1 More thought should perhaps be given to the recruitment and/or training of the systems analysts.
2 Stricter adherence to the standards laid down to guide the analysts in their work may be called for.
3 Closer involvement of the EDP department's management in the work of the analyst will help; regular progress meetings should be held so that work can be monitored.
4 Closer involvement of the auditor and the staff of the user department at all stages, particularly systems testing, will be fruitful.
5 Rigid enforcement of documentation standards should be one of management's priorities.

26.6 Faulty programming

Program bugs are a very common cause of errors in the results produced by computer systems. Once again, strict adherence to standards, with the emphasis on checking and re-checking at all stages of the programmer's work, will help to reduce the incidence of such bugs. The stages of program testing and system testing are, clearly, crucial.

26.7 Errors by the operator

If an operator loses some of the data which should be read into a computer system as part of a transactions file, or if the wrong version of a master file is loaded onto a disk drive for reading by an update program, then disastrous errors can be the result.

The likelihood of such 'mis-ops' happening can be reduced by:

1 Strict adherence to the standards laid down to guide the work of the operators.

2 Careful use of the operating instructions which the analyst will have drawn up to inform the operators about the specific system they are running. In particular, the security provisions, such as dumping and logging, or sending copies of master files to remote locations, must be rigidly adhered to.

3 Systems design which takes account of the possibility of such errors and builds in checks which attempt to prevent them.

4 The use of header labels and write permit rings.

26.8   Errors in the input

This is a second very common cause of errors. The steps to be taken in an attempt to prevent inaccurate results being produced are:

1 Careful visual scrutiny of source documents in the department that originates them.

2 Verification; the process of verifying was explained at length in Chapter 4.

3 Checks in the validate program, including the use of batch control records (see Chapter 19).

4 Checks in the update program (see Chapter 19).

5 Strict adherence to the standards laid down to guide the work of the data control clerks who were discussed in Chapter 23.

26.9   Fraud

In an attempt to safeguard a computer system against deliberate efforts fraudulently to abuse it, the following methods can be used:

1 Identification of the users of remote terminals by such methods as badges, passwords and the use of interrogation questions to which only the authorized user is likely to know the correct answers. Locks on doors, of course, should not be overlooked!

2 Important files and documents should be kept in safes.

3 Precautions can be taken against wire-tapping, and encryption of data can make industrial espionage more difficult.

26.10 Physical security

There are many well-documented cases of companies suffering greatly because catastrophies such as fires, burst pipes or even sabotage have created havoc in their EDP departments. Such precautions as the use of fire-proof safes and of efficient alarm systems should be used so as to minimize the losses which would be suffered under these circumstances.

Bypass procedures, which perhaps allow transactions to be recorded off-line when the computer system is out of action, should be built into a real-time system. This will allow some sort of service to be given at all times.

Alternative processing facilities, perhaps at the installation of another user who has a similar configuration, will help during computer downtime.

In extreme circumstances, twin processing systems may be justified. These involve the use of two computers which run in parallel, and thus give cover to each other. Clearly, this approach gives good protection to the user, but is enormously expensive.

26.11 The auditor

26.11.1 The role of the auditor

It is the responsibility of the auditor to determine whether or not an organization's assets are properly protected. Having looked at the possible sources of errors in computerized systems, and bearing in mind the fact that there is always the possibility of deliberate fraud, we are now in a position to examine the problems faced by the auditor when concerned with an electronic data processing system, and the methods used to overcome those problems.

26.11.2 Problems posed by the computer

When a manual data processing system has been properly developed and is being operated efficiently, the auditor's task is a fairly straightforward one; procedures are well-documented, hard copies of all transactions are available, an audit trail can be followed, and duties will be separated so as to minimize the possibility of collusion and fraud. But when data processing is carried out electronically, special problems are faced by an auditor:

1 The auditor may lack knowledge of computer terms and concepts, and may thus be unaware of how to adapt to the new methods of working.

2 The computer personnel responsible for developing the new systems will probably know little about accountancy, auditing, or the legal framework within which their systems are to operate; this may lead to problems.

3 Once data processing is computerized, it often becomes centralized as well. This means that one traditional safeguard against error and fraud — the principle of the segregation of duties — is lost, because the computer carries out all the required tasks.

4 The previous point is exacerbated by the fact that computer processing is automatic; this means that human 'common sense' checks cannot easily be built into the system.

5 An audit trail will be difficult to follow when processing is computerized, for the following reasons:

(a) data within a computer system is 'invisible' to the human being, as it is kept in machine-sensible form;

(b) many computer systems, in order to reduce processing costs, do not hold historical data in the way that many manual systems do;

(c) because transactions are usually sorted by program within the computer system, the source documents which give rise to those transactions do not need to be sorted; they are thus often held in haphazard order which makes retrieval of individual records more difficult;

(d) the exception principle is often used, and this means that the vast majority of transactions may not be printed out.

6 Real-time systems pose special problems. Because data originates at remote locations, transactions are more difficult to check, and the problems are increased when, for example, orders received over the telephone are input directly to a computer system without a hard-copy being made. Unauthorized use of a terminal can also cause difficulties. 'Pipeline' problems arise when a real-time system fails while transactions are being dealt with; has the master file been updated or not?

The above problems mean that a computer system, if no special action is taken, will be difficult, if not impossible, to audit adequately. In particular, the auditor must verify:

- that the design of the system itself is sound, and
- given a sound system, that the day-to-day running of that system is being properly carried out

26.11.3 Solutions to the problems

Several steps can be taken by the auditor in an attempt to overcome the special problems posed by computerized data processing systems. Some of them are:

1 The auditors must acquire a working knowledge of EDP and its ramifications. It is useful for at least one member of an audit team to have extensive first-hand experience of computing.

2 A sound working relationship must be established with the computer department's personnel, and the EDP staff must be convinced that the auditors have a useful contribution to make.

3 The auditors must take an active role, rather than a passive one, when a new system is being developed, or an existing system is being modified. This will enable them to ensure, for example, that adequate use is being made of batch control totals; subsequent changes, after all, will prove expensive. In particular, the auditors need to be involved at the following stages:

- the project feasibility study
- systems design
- program testing and system testing
- implementation of the system

4 The auditors should insist on a strict segregation of duties. The functions identified in Chapter 23 should be carried out by different individuals in order to prevent collusion.

5 An approach known as 'auditing round the computer' can be employed. This involves treating the computer as a 'black box'; the auditor is not concerned with what happens inside the box, (s)he merely checks that the output is consistent with the input. This approach requires less computer knowledge on the part of the auditor, and may well be effective for simple systems.

6 An audit trail can be created where one does not already exist. Printouts can be requested on a regular or an ad hoc basis, either

of exceptional items or at random. This will allow the auditors to check that transactions are correctly actioned.

7 The auditors may use specially-created test packs to test a system. These packs will probably consist of real data alongside artificial transactions and, when put through the system, they will enable the auditor to determine whether the data has been correctly processed and whether deliberately-inserted errors have been detected. Such a test pack can be created during the system testing stage and, once built-up, can be re-used whenever the system is modified, or whenever a spot check on its accuracy is required.

8 Standard audit packages are available which:
(a) allow random sampling of the contents of a file, perhaps printing every nth record;
(b) cause exceptional items to be printed;
(c) give control totals of certain important fields. Where such packages are not available, they can be written internally.

9 Spot checks on the computer installation, and on certain systems which run on the computer, should be made. These will allow the auditors to ensure that standards are being adhered to in all areas – analysis, programming, operations, the library, data preparation and data control – and that, in particular, documentation standards are being enforced. Copies of all documents produced in the computer department, specifications, manuals, logs and so on, should be taken away for scrutiny by the auditors. Visits to the EDP department will enable auditors to see whether the duties in the department are indeed segregated in practice.

10 Special care should be taken with real-time systems. Auditors should check that unauthorized access is not being made to the system, and spot checks can be carried out by logging transactions for a period and following-up each of them. Visits may be made unannounced to the locations from which entries to the system are made.

11 Questionnaires and checklists can be used by the auditors to ensure that all aspects of control are covered.

12 Throughout their work, the auditors must ask questions. Experience will often allow them to sense whether or not something is wrong with a system.

Examination questions

1 A construction and civil engineering company, operating on a dozen or so sites spread over most of the United Kingdom, has

decided that, as its first computer job, it will take on the payroll. The company auditors have expressed some concern regarding the proposed operation.

As data processing manager, prepare a report to the auditors explaining the audit and control features which are to be incorporated into the new system.

(Institute of Cost and Management Accountants)

2 What special problems are faced by the auditor when dealing with computerized systems? How can (s)he attempt to overcome these problems?

3 Describe the principal organizational and staffing controls that should be present in a computer department.

Certain error conditions are always likely to occur during updating, when transactions are being applied to a master file.

Identify and briefly explain four different error situation reports which would typically be incorporated in a computer-based stock control system and which might occur as output when stock records are being updated with transaction data.

(Chartered Association of Certified Accountants)

27

The legal implications of computer use

27.1 Introduction
27.2 The Data Protection Act 1984
27.3 The Computer Misuse Act 1990
Questions

27.1 Introduction

As we have seen throughout this text, because of its speed and its power, and because of its ability to be linked with other processors and data banks in massive networks, the computer offers huge benefits to its users. Unfortunately, the computerization of an organization's operations also leads to new problems, particularly in the areas of privacy of information and the misuse of files and programs.

This chapter looks briefly at the provisions of two pieces of legislation which are relevant to computer use, and at some of their implications. As such, the chapter is of vital importance to all users of computers, to managers who are responsible for staff who use computers and to accountants, auditors and others.

27.2 The Data Protection Act 1984

27.2.1 Introduction

The act was passed in order to satisfy two objectives:

1 To protect individuals from the misuse of computers. The fear is that data concerning individuals which is held on computer files can be processed and transferred at great speed, and that individuals can suffer if such data is inaccurate or is passed to a third party who has no right to see it. In an attempt to deal with this, the act lays down a set of standards for the computerized processing of data concerning individuals.

2   To allow the UK to ratify the 'Council of Europe Convention for the Protection of Individuals with Regard to the Automatic Processing of Personal Data'. If this were not done, then data could not flow freely between the UK and other European countries, and damage could thus be done to the UK's international trade.

Note that the act only applies to automatically-processed data about living and identifiable human beings. It does not cover data concerning companies or other entities, and it does not apply to manual systems.

27.2.2   The provisions of the Data Protection Act

1   The act sets up a public **register** of both **data users** and **computer bureaux**. A data user is a person or organization who controls and uses a file of personal data which is capable of being processed automatically, for example by computer. Unless they are specifically exempted, such users have to register under the act with the Data Protection Registrar, and they have to abide by the data protection principles which are laid down in the act.

When they register, data users must supply:

● their name and address
● a description of the data which they hold, and of the uses to which it is put
● a description of the sources of the data, and of the recipients of the data, including any overseas countries to which it is transferred
● the name and address of the person to whom individuals may write in order to gain access to their data

Once they have registered, data users must not do anything which is not covered by their register entry, and they must only disclose data to people described in the register entry, and to the individual whom the data concerns.

A computer bureau is a person or organization who processes personal data on a computer for data users, or who allows third parties to use its equipment for the processing of such data. Bureaux need to register with the Registrar, but they need only supply their name and address.

Bureaux must abide by the data protection principles, and must take adequate security precautions regarding the personal data which is held.

An individual may be entitled to compensation if a bureau fails to abide by the act.

2   The act gives **data subjects**, that is the individuals about whom data is held, the right of access to that data, and the right to have it corrected or erased in certain circumstances. A data subject may enquire of a data user as to whether or not the user holds personal data about him/her on a computer file. If such data is held, then, upon payment of a reasonable fee, the data user must supply the data subject with an intelligible copy of that data within 40 days.

If a data subject suffers damage because of inaccurate data or inadequately-protected data, then (s)he is entitled to compensation. The data subject has the right to have inaccurate data, or data held in breach of the data protection principles, corrected or erased.

3   The **Data Protection Registrar** is charged with the administration of the act. The Registrar has the authority to investigate complaints and to:

(a)   issue an **enforcement notice** which forces a data user to comply with the act, for example by making the user erase or correct inaccurate data;

(b)   prevent a data user from transferring data overseas, by use of a **transfer prohibition notice**, if it is felt that such a transfer could lead to a breach of the data protection principles;

(c)   debar a data user from holding personal data by issuing a **deregistration notice**.

4   A data user may appeal to the **Data Protection Tribunal** if he or she feels unjustly dealt with by the Registrar.

5   The eight principles of data protection are internationally agreed:

(a)   data must have been obtained fairly and lawfully;

(b)   it must be used only for the purposes described in the data user's register entry;

(c)   it must only be disclosed in accordance with the user's register entry;

(d)   it must be adequate for, relevant to and not excessive for the purpose(s) stated in the register entry;

(e)   it must be accurate and up-to-date;

(f)   it must not be kept for longer than is necessary for the stated purpose(s);

(g)   it must be disclosed to the data subject on request;

(h)   it must be protected against loss or unauthorized disclosure.

6 In the following circumstances, a data user is exempt from registering under the act:
(a)   data held for national security;
(b)   data held only for accounting or payroll purposes, although there are disclosure restrictions;
(c)   data which has to be made publicly available according to law;
(d)   data held only for the production of documents on such systems as word processors;
(e)   mailing lists consisting of only names and addresses;
(f)   data held by unincorporated clubs about their members, but only if the members have not objected: there are disclosure restrictions;
(g)   data held purely for recreational or domestic purposes.

7   Subject access need not be given in the following circumstances:
(a)   data held for law enforcement or revenue purposes, where access would damage those purposes;
(b)   legally-privileged data;
(c)   data held for back-up purposes;
(d)   data held so that the providers of financial services can be regulated;
(e)   data relating to judicial appointments;
(f)   data held for research purposes, provided that individuals cannot be identified from any disclosed data.

8   Data can be disclosed, even if the disclosure is not permitted under the register entry, in the following circumstances:
(a)   law enforcement or revenue purposes;
(b)   in cases involving national security;
(c)   where disclosure is legally required;
(d)   urgent disclosure to prevent damage to health;
(e)   where the data subject has consented.

The above summary of the Data Protection Act is based upon guidelines issued by the Data Protection Registrar but, of course, it does not attempt to be a definite statement of what the act says – only the act itself is authoritative. Further information can be obtained from:

The Office of the Data Protection Registrar
Springfield House
Water Lane
Wilmslow
Cheshire
SK9 5AX

27.2.3   The implications of the Data Protection Act

1   Although individuals are given certain rights under the act, the Registrar's staff of less than one hundred people have hundreds of thousands of registrations to deal with. Until the act has been in operation for a number of years, therefore, it is difficult to see how effective it will be.

2   The act makes it illegal to hold personal data without the data user being registered, and it is illegal to use the data for purposes not covered by the register entry.

3   Because of this, organizations holding personal data on computer files will have to take careful precautions to ensure that the act is being correctly complied with. The appointment of a data protection co-ordinator to ensure that all the organization's staff are conversant with the provisions of the act, and that they are complying with it, is the least that should be done.

4   The role of the co-ordinator will be an ongoing one, as (s)he will have to monitor the organization's operations in relation to the act, perhaps in order to amend the register entry if procedures change, and ensure that new employees know of its implications. A periodic 'census' of what staff are doing − including the use of microcomputers, of course − is called for.

Co-ordinators will also have to keep themselves informed of anything published by the Registrar, and of any court judgements concerning the act.

5   All of the above will involve the data user in some expense, although one practical benefit should be tighter control of data.

27.3   The Computer Misuse Act 1990

27.3.1   Introduction

The Computer Misuse Act 1990 was introduced in order to combat the widespread, deliberate misuse of computer systems. Thus the act covers such practices as:

- 'hacking' into a system in order to view sensitive data or alter that data
- stealing computer time in order to carry out unauthorized work
- copying computer programs without proper authority

- implanting 'viruses' into systems, so that files or programs are mutilated or destroyed
- entering bogus records onto a computer file, so that payments are made, for example to non-existent suppliers
- altering delivery addresses, so that goods can be diverted
- and many others.

27.3.2 The provisions of the Computer Misuse Act

The act tries to define what is meant by computer misuse, and it lays down penalties for such misuse. Three new offences are introduced:

- unauthorized access to computer material
- unauthorized access with intent to facilitate commission of further offences
- unauthorized modification of computer material

Each of these is briefly discussed in the sections which follow.

1 Unauthorized access to computer material It is an offence deliberately to attempt to gain unauthorized access to data and/or programs held in a computer. The offence is committed whether or not the attempt is successful, and whether or not any data or programs are actually changed. A person who knowingly exceeds his or her authorized access limits commits an offence. Piracy of programs, already the civil offence of breach of copyright, is an offence.

2 Unauthorized access with intent to commit or facilitate further offences This covers an offence under 1 above, which is committed in order to carry out, for example, a serious fraud. The further offence need not be by the same person, nor need it be at the same time. The offence is still committed even though the further crime did not succeed: it is immaterial whether or not the further crime was technically possible.

3 Unauthorized modification of computer material It is an offence deliberately to modify or erase the programs or data in a computer, to impair the operation of a computer or system, to hinder access to a system, or to affect the reliability of the system or the data. This section clearly covers viruses and the like, but it also covers unauthorized modification by an authorized user.

27.3.3 The implications of the Computer Misuse Act

The penalty for unauthorized access is up to six months imprisonment and a £2000 fine. The other offences carry up to five years imprisonment and an unlimited fine.

It is important that all users of computers, managers who are responsible for staff who use computers, and accountants, auditors and others are informed abut the act, in terms of its requirements and the associated penalties. In many organizations today, this will mean almost every member of staff.

Adequate control measures must be put into place in a computer-using organization, and action must be taken to remedy any weaknesses in procedures which could lead to contravention of the act.

The working of the act, and any court judgements made, should be carefully monitored over time.

Examination questions

1 What are the implications of the Data Protection Act for a large company which uses distributed data processing? What steps should be taken to ensure that the act is complied with?

2 Explain why legislation such as the Computer Misuse Act is needed, given the ways in which information technology is used in the 1990s.

3 How does the Computer Misuse Act attempt to combat the deliberate misuse of computer systems? What are its implications for the manager?

28

Some social implications of computer use

28.1 Introduction
28.2 Automation
28.3 Privacy
28.4 Summary
   Question

28.1 Introduction

Because of its ability to input and process vast amounts of data repetitively and accurately, and because it can very rapidly retrieve single items of data from high-volume files, the computer undoubtedly bestows many advantages on the human race. In industry and commerce, much routine manual work which was formerly carried out by armies of human beings can be eliminated; this increases productivity and accuracy, lowers costs, and can lead to lower prices and an increase in the quality of the service rendered to the customer. In such diverse areas as law, medicine, education, traffic control and meteorology, the computer is also being increasingly used to great advantage.

This second industrial revolution, however, has not been universally welcomed by all who have witnessed it. In this final chapter we briefly examine two of the social issues raised by the use of the computer.

28.2 Automation

The replacement of human workers by the computer is an example of automation. Whether this automation takes place in the office or on the shop-floor, it must result in redundancies and some technological unemployment, with potentially very great repercussions.

To date, widespread unemployment has not resulted from the introduction of computerized systems. This is because the computer often creates as many jobs as it saves, and thus an opportunity arises for re-training replaced staff. Another relevant factor is that the type of workers who are replaced by the computers are in the grades of labour which, in any case, exhibit high rates of labour turnover; 'silent firing' or natural wastage can thus often take care of staff surpluses.

In the future, however, the decreasing cost of computer hardware and the increased use of microprocessors can only add to the problem of unemployment, and the effects of the computer will be felt most strongly by those least able to cope with those effects, i.e. the unskilled. Clearly, society will have to re-think fundamentally its attitudes to work and leisure.

28.3   Privacy

Government bodies and private organizations have been collecting and holding data about individuals for many years. In the days before the advent of the computer, few people thought that files of data concerning taxation, social security, driving licences or legal affairs posed a threat, but many people view these matters somewhat differently today.

The problem is, of course, that advances in computer technology have made it far easier for organizations to collect and hold vast amounts of data, and far easier for that data to be disseminated. In particular, the following points are causing concern to many people:

1   Data which has been collected legitimately for a given purpose may be abused by the organization holding it.
2   An organization holding data may sell it to an unscrupulous third party, without the consent, or even the knowledge, of the individuals to whom it relates.
3   Data held in a data bank may not be secure against attempts made by a determined third party to access that data.
4   Data stored in a data bank may contain errors. This may, in extreme cases, cause a request for a loan to be refused, or an application for a job to be rejected.
5   If some sort of standard universal identifying number were issues to every citizen, it could be used as the key field for the records on many different data banks. This in effect, would allow many different data banks to be linked together, so that the total picture concerning an individual could be seen. This, clearly, could have sinister implications.

6 Computer systems can be misused by unscrupulous individuals in various ways, ranging from 'hacking' to software piracy. The Data Protection Act and the Computer Misuse Act are, clearly, attempts to overcome some of these problems.

28.4 Summary

The increasing use of computers in commercial and industrial organizations has posed and is posing new problems, among which are problems concerning automation, privacy and misuse.

Examination question

1 What problems concerning privacy are posed by the increasing use of the computer? What legislative remedies are available?

Appendix

Answers to selected questions

Chapter 18

1	T
3	F
5	F
7	T
9	(d)
11	(d).

Chapter 19

1	T
3	F
5	F
7	T
9	T
11	F
13	T
15	T
17	T
19	T
21	(c)
23	(d)
25	(c)

Index

Whatever software package you are learning ...

- Aldus PageMaker
- dBase III
- dBase IV
- DataEase 4
- Locoscript 1 & 2
- Lotus 1-2-3
- Microsoft Word for Windows
- MS-DOS
- Multiplan
- Pegasus
- Paradox
- Sage Bookkeeper

- Smartware 1
- Supercalc 5
- Symphony 2
- Timeworks Publisher 2
- Ventura Publisher
- UNIX
- WordPerfect 5.0
- Wordperfect 5.1
- Wordstar 4
- Wordstar 1512
- Wordwise

etc

You will find a book in the *Training Guide* series suited to your needs.

Each title follows the same, effective format:

- the text is fully comprehensive yet free of jargon
- instructions are carefully structured
- covers all main functions of the package
- tasks and activities teach the various commands and reinforce learning

Ask for the titles in the *Training Guide* series in your local bookstore. Alternatively, contact our marketing department: **Pitman Publishing,** 128 Long Acre, London WC2E 9AN. Telephone: 071-379 7383.

From Start to Finish Series

This major new series offers its readers complete and thorough mastery of the most widely used databases, spreadsheets and word processing packages.

Suitable for use by absolute beginners, each title will take the student through every aspect of the package until they have achieved a significant level of competence. The format and structure of the books enable students to follow one learning strategy (and use only one book) for preparation for the series of examinations they need to pass

- covers all functions and applications of each package
- geared to the needs of the student who wishes to pass examinations after each learning stage
- a one-book solution to learning a package from elementary to advanced levels
- accompanying 3.5″ and 5.25″ disks are available for each title

Titles include:

From Start to Finish: dBASE IV 1.1
From Start to Finish: Lotus for Windows
From Start to Finish: Microsoft Word for Windows
From Start to Finish: WordPerfect for Windows

Ask for the titles in the *From Start to Finish* series in your local bookstore. Alternatively, contact our marketing department. **Pitman Publishing**, 128 Long Acre, London WC2E 9AN.
Telephone: 071-379 7383

Each Access Series

EASY ACCESS texts provide complete introductions to popular word processing packages.

The reader is taken from basic to intermediate level with a series of simple modules which have supporting exercises to give hands-on consolidation and revision. Advanced material is also included in some texts where indicated.

EASY ACCESS texts are ideal for first-time computer users, whether in academic, commercial or home surroundings. In particular, the series provides excellent examination preparation for the practical components of exams set by the RSA, LCCI, PEI and other similar bodies. All the texts are written by experienced lecturers.

- easy-to-follow and user friendly, including helpful use of mnemonics
- each section is carefully structured
- ideal for both academic and commercial use
- written by experienced lecturers in word processing
- supporting exercises to give hands-on consolidation and revision

In addition to word processing software instructions, each guide contains:

- sufficient notes on the operating systems, e.g. DOS, to meet everyday system housekeeping requirements
- a glossary of terms to assist the uninitiated through an area which is sometimes fogbound with jargon
- tips on suggested applications to assist and encourage the reader to obtain the maximum use of the features available in the word processing software package.

Titles include:

Easy Access to DisplayWrite 4 & 5
Easy Access to Locoscript 1
Easy Access to Locoscript 2
Easy Access to Microscoft Word 4 & 5
Easy Access to WordPerfect 4.2 incorporating V 4.1 and 5.0
Easy Access to WordStar Book 1 & Book 2, V 2 and 3
Easy Access to WordStar Professional 4 & 5
Easy Access to Wordwise

Ask for the titles in the *Easy Access* series in your local bookstore. Alternatively, contact our marketing department: **Pitman Publishing**, 128 Long Acre, London WC2E 9AN. Telephone: 071-379 7383

Open Learning Series

An increasing number of people are developing word processing skills in the confines of their home or office and are sitting their final examination as an outside student entry. Many college courses are now also based upon open learning techniques. This user-friendly series provides clear and step-by-step instruction to all aspects of each package.

- purpose-written open learning material
- user-friendly, with helpful guidance notes
- clear, easy-to-follow instructions
- logical and consistent layout offering concise and effective instruction
- each unit is self-contained to allow 'dip-in' learning for those requiring revision within certain areas of application.

Titles include:

Microsoft Word 5.5
WordPerfect 5.1

Ask for the titles in the *Open Learning* series in your local bookstore. Alternatively, contact our marketing department: **Pitman Publishing**, 128 Long Acre, London WC2E 9AN. Telephone: 071-379 7383